GETTYSBURG

IN ART AND ARTIFACTS

TREASURES FROM THE GETTYSBURG NATIONAL PARK MUSEUM
AND VISITOR CENTER

ARTWORK BY KEITH ROCCO
WRITTEN BY ROBERT I. GIRARDI

Crimson Books

First published in the United States of America in 2010 by Crimson Books, Inc.
440 Thomas Avenue, Forest Park, IL, 60130, USA
www.crimsonbooksinc.com

ISBN-13: 978-0-9841652-2-3 Soft cover edition
ISBN-13: 978-0-9841652-3-0 Hard cover edition

Edited by Lynda Fitzgerald
Print Management and Design by HeuleGordon, Inc.
Printed and bound in China
Copyright ©2010

GETTYSBURG

IN ART AND ARTIFACTS

TREASURES FROM THE GETTYSBURG NATIONAL PARK MUSEUM
AND VISITOR CENTER

ACKNOWLEDGEMENTS

No book could be completed without the assistance of many skilled people who gave generously of their time and expertise. Greg Goodell, John Heiser and Scott Hartwig, of Gettysburg National Military Park all gave great assistance, taking time from their busy schedules to answer questions and provide helpful tips and suggestions. Sue Boardman, a licensed battlefield guide read the manuscript and helped to clear up some misconceptions and misstatements. Thanks to the design team at Heule-Gordon Inc., especially to Tiffany Sinkule, who did great service in laying out the book and revising each and every image. Will Hutchinson of Gettysburg lent his time, energy and equipment to help photograph the artifacts and images included herein. Jeff Clinedinst of J. Clinedinst Photography used his technical skills to perfect the artifacts and images for publication. Paula C. Walker and Lynda Fitzgerald, and Fred and Anne Henders proofread the manuscript for clarity and consistency. Joe Abboreno, of Abboreno Studios provided the maps. Without this team of friendly and skilled men and women, this book would not have come to fruition. Finally, we would like to thank the National Park Service for the use of their images of the art and artifacts.

❧ INTRODUCTION ❧

The McPherson Farm

On July 1, 1863 two massive armies made their way to the crossroads town of Gettysburg, Pennsylvania and engaged in an unplanned epic battle. The battle defined the war, played a key role in its outcome, and the commemoration of it helped to bring the divided nation back together in a spirit of shared sacrifice and reconciliation. A few months after the battle, President Abraham Lincoln immortalized the memory of Gettysburg in his most famous speech.

Gettysburg is compellingly a story of America. Here the valor, bravery and courage of the Civil War are on display, together with the savage violence, ferocious devotion to ideals and cause and acts of selfless bravery and humanity as the combatants struggled both during the battle and in its aftermath. Gettysburg is an episode in our history both wonderful and terrible. Today, when looking over the beautifully sculpted landscape of farms and fields, hills, streams and wooded lots, it seems a travesty to think of the massive violence enacted here over the course of three July days in 1863. Yet marble and granite monuments testify to the magnitude and importance of the events of those three days. And the thousands of soldiers' graves in the National Cemetery provide mute testimony to the cost of the battle.

The vastness of Gettysburg is almost too much for one to comprehend. The terrible battle was the largest and costliest ever fought on North American soil. Its sweeping drama, tragedy and heroism are nearly mythic in proportion and are compelling enough to draw millions of visitors to the battleground and even more readers to the thousands of books written on the subject. To understand the war, one must study Gettysburg. Gettysburg is the Civil War.

It is not enough, however, to look at just the commanding generals or the pivotal battlegrounds. One must also turn to the individuals, be they privates, non-commissioned officers or line officers. And to put the meaning of the battle into a larger context, one must also study the commemoration of that battleground to understand its significance not only to the veterans, but also to those drawn there today.

Federal 6th Corps infantry officer

Gettysburg is hallowed ground. It is America. It is a vital, living reminder of the sacrifices of the past. Those dead buried in the National Cemetery at Gettysburg did not die in vain. As long as these fields are preserved, every visitor from home or abroad, can come and study, see where great deeds were done and sense the power that the past continues to exert over the present. It is the effort to understand and tap into this power that fuels our desire to study history. In the words of Joshua Lawrence Chamberlain, the divinity teacher and commander of the 20th Maine Volunteer Infantry, who is credited with saving the Federal left flank on Little Round Top, *"In great deeds, something abides. On great fields something stays. Forms change and pass; bodies disappear, but spirits linger, to consecrate the ground for the vision-place of souls. And reverent men and women from afar, and generations that know us not and that we know not of, heart-drawn to see where and by whom great things were suffered and done for them shall come to this deathless field to ponder and dream; And lo!, the shadow of a mighty presence shall wrap them in its bosom, and the power of the vision pass into their souls."* These eloquent and prophetic words aptly describe both the meaning and the importance of coming to a battlefield like Gettysburg. The past speaks to us through the rocks and trees, in the

Confederate infantry bugler

words carved into stone or cast in bronze, in the grim visages of the monuments and the solemn silence of the cemetery.

This book is not intended to be a comprehensive history of the battle; rather it is an overview, highlighting some of the events and persons who participated in the struggle. The story is presented in words, photographs, art and artifacts from the battlefield and from the collections of the Gettysburg Museum. The artifacts are not merely witnesses, but active participants of the battle, bringing it to life in a tangible sense. They are a visual and tactile bridge to the past. Keith Rocco's art adds to this dimension, providing colorful imagery of the men and the scenes of battle, depicting historic events as they may have appeared to those present. The combination of art and artifacts, word and images, tell the story of Gettysburg in a new way, focusing on the people who were there. Each soldier, each person who participated in these events matters as much now as then. It is important for us to respect and appreciate the sacrifices of those who came before us. Their efforts mirror our own struggles, making their lives more relevant to us, the distant consumers of history.

Artist Keith Rocco has made a career of presenting the war from the point of view of the common soldier. The power of his style brings the action in his canvasses to life, placing the viewer directly into the action. His work is filled with emotion, neither glorifying nor editorializing the war, simply presenting episodes of it in a gripping manner, giving one interpretation of the view of the action as experienced by those involved in it. This volume contains some of his best work on the Battle of Gettysburg, including several new paintings created specifically for this book.

Author and historian Robert I. Girardi has produced numerous works that deal with the personal experience of the leaders and the soldiers who fought the Civil War. He has worked with Rocco for many years and the two together have the same perspective when dealing with the presentation of the soldier's view. Once again these two team up to present a unique view of Gettysburg.

❧ PREFACE ❧
THE GETTYSBURG MUSEUM
AN INTERVIEW WITH GREG GOODELL

WHAT IS YOUR JOB TITLE? LENGTH OF TIME IN THAT POSITION?

I am the Chief of Museum Services and I have been at Gettysburg since 2001. As such, I have the responsibility for the overall management of Gettysburg National Military Park's archival and artifact collections.

DESCRIBE THE SCOPE OF THE GETTYSBURG COLLECTIONS.

The archival and museum collections of the park number over one million individual items. As you can imagine, a collection like this is very broad in its coverage. It contains flags, uniforms, equipment, letters, diaries, maps, monument sketches, photographs, archeological collections, artillery tubes and projectiles, musical instruments, and furniture. What ties all of these varied items together is the common thread of the battle of Gettysburg, the overall history of the Civil War, or the creation of the commemorative landscape that is Gettysburg National Military Park.

The collecting and exhibit of historical objects at Gettysburg began right after the guns fell silent. The earliest preservation organization on the battlefield, the Gettysburg Battlefield Memorial Association, was established in 1864 to begin preserving key parts of the battlefield for posterity. One of the first pieces of property that the GBMA purchased was General Meade's headquarters (the Leister House). It was there that the organization displayed a small number of battlefield relics for visitors to see. As the federal government became increasingly involved in the management and administration of the battlefield after 1895 (when the park was formally created under the U.S. War Department), it too began to accumulate small numbers of artifacts to enhance its interpretive activities. By 1970, the National Park Service (which assumed administration of the park in 1933) had assembled a small collection of significant battle-related artifacts, including the world-famous Cyclorama Painting of Pickett's Charge, that it used to help visitors better understand the events of the battle.

In 1971 the park would receive its largest single collection and, with it, the ability to change the nature of museums in Gettysburg. This was the Rosensteel Collection. Started by young John Rosensteel immediately following the battle and enhanced with acquisitions by his family and descendents, it consisted of Gettysburg battlefield relics, original Civil War uniforms and equipment, and significant artifacts from other parts of the conflict. The Rosensteel family operated a private museum in Gettysburg where they displayed these collections for all Gettysburg visitors to see. In 1971, the National Park Service negotiated the purchase of this museum building and land and, with that purchase, received the entire artifact collection it contained. This core collection really enhanced the ability of the NPS to tell the story of the entire Civil War and not just the story of Gettysburg.

By no means did the National Park Service stop collecting artifacts following this important acquisition. From 1971 to the present day, the NPS at Gettysburg has collected (mostly through donations by individual members of the public and park support organizations) thousands of additional items to enhance its interpretive mission. Many of these artifacts have a particular provenance to individuals or known events. The result is that today, the park's holds the largest public collection of Civil War artifacts in the nation.

WHAT ARE SOME OF THE PARTICULAR TREASURES OF THE COLLECTION?

The greatest treasure in the collection is the Cyclorama Painting, which has just undergone a multi-million dollar restoration. Other highlights of the collection

*Confederate slouch hat,
tarred for weather-proofing .*

A mannequin of a Federal cavalryman with all of his accouterments stands in the Gettysburg Visitor Center.

include significant pieces that tell very interesting and detailed stories about the battle and the Civil War. One is the very first map made of the battlefield (made in the fall of 1863) by Topographical engineer Emmor B. Cope. Cope would later become the park engineer under the War Department and have a significant role in creating the park's built environment. Another is one of the swords of General George G. Meade, donated to the park by the General's grandson. Still another is the dress frock coat of Confederate General James Pettigrew, killed at the end of the Gettysburg campaign and Falling Waters, as the Army of Northern Virginia was withdrawing across the Potomac River. There is the remnants of the litter used to carry a wounded Stonewall Jackson off the field during the Battle of Chancellorsville. Finally, there is the furniture from the bedroom of the David Wills House in which President Lincoln slept and where he put the finishing touches on the Gettysburg Address. There are, of course, many items in the collection that are not as storied as these. But, no matter how large or small, each item has a certain level of significance and contributes to our understanding of the battle and of the war.

How can artifacts help us to understand and interpret the battle of Gettysburg?

Artifacts are an important tool that we use to understand and interpret the battle at Gettysburg. An object is a tangible link to an individual and an event. Visitors really respond to seeing that flag that was carried during Pickett's Charge, or that sharpshooter rifle left behind in Devil's Den, or that drum

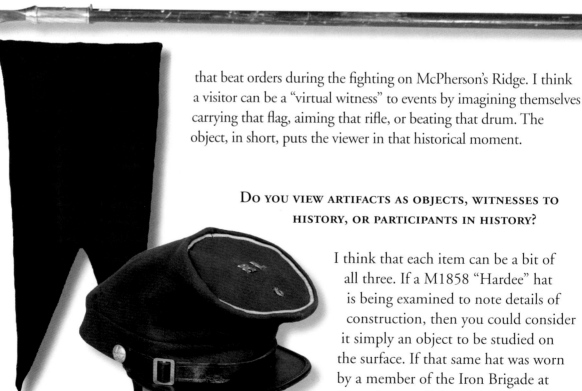

that beat orders during the fighting on McPherson's Ridge. I think a visitor can be a "virtual witness" to events by imagining themselves carrying that flag, aiming that rifle, or beating that drum. The object, in short, puts the viewer in that historical moment.

Do you view artifacts as objects, witnesses to history, or participants in history?

I think that each item can be a bit of all three. If a M1858 "Hardee" hat is being examined to note details of construction, then you could consider it simply an object to be studied on the surface. If that same hat was worn by a member of the Iron Brigade at Gettysburg on July 1st (and we have the documentation to prove that), then that same hat has both "witnessed" and "participated" in that historical event.

6th Pennsylvania Cavalry, Rush's Lancers, kepi, lance and guidon. Rush's Lancers was an elite regiment from Philadelphia.

The focus of the museum is to highlight the participants and events of the Battle of Gettysburg and to place these within the larger context of the overall War and, more importantly, within the larger context of American history. In terms of to whom it is geared, the answer is that we have tried to gear it to everyone! Gettysburg is a destination for a wide ranging audience that wants to learn different things in different ways. Therefore, we have attempted to meet the needs of all visitors to the museum. For example, we hope that first-time visitors gain a general understanding of the Civil War by experiencing the exhibits in the main galleries. Artifact selection is therefore more broad and wide-ranging in order to convey the most critical overarching themes of the battle and the war. Computer interactives also form a facet of this learning experience. Almost all museums that are designed today have a strong computer interactive component as part of their make-up. Younger visitors are very technically aware and respond very favorably to these types of exhibits. We also recognize that Gettysburg has a very large audience of returning visitors and more serious students of the material culture of the Civil War, particularly its military aspects. We use the concept of "open storage" to engage these returning visitors and collectors. This "open storage" is a relatively new phenomena in museums, but one that is making its mark in places like the Smithsonian and the New York Historical Society, to name a few. In the case of Gettysburg, our "open storage" gives the opportunity for a closer, more thorough examination of military artifacts and weaponry than what can be gained in the main museum galleries. The museum at the park really has to meet the needs of the largest number of visitors and the largest number of learning styles.

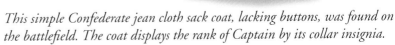

This simple Confederate jean cloth sack coat, lacking buttons, was found on the battlefield. The coat displays the rank of Captain by its collar insignia.

THE
GETTYSBURG CAMPAIGN

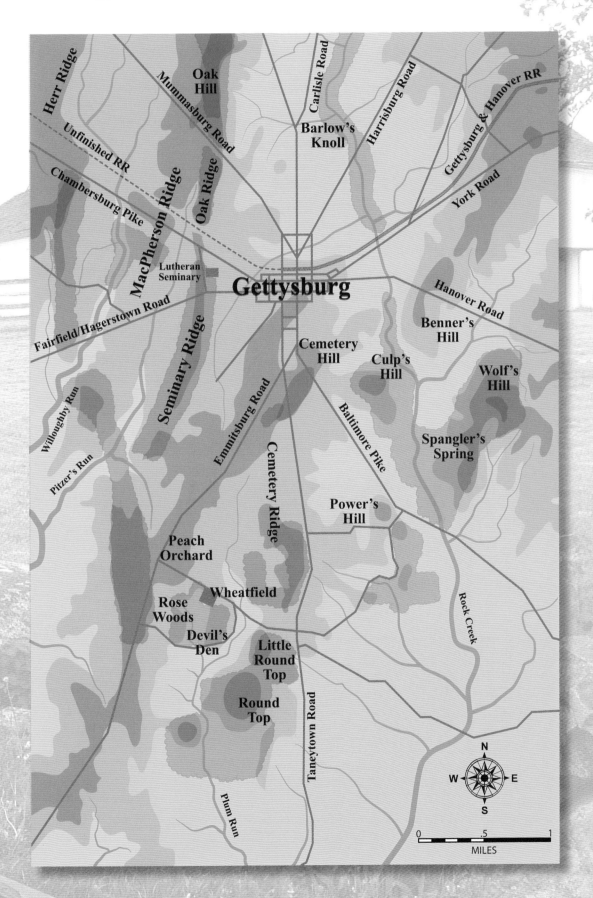

Herr Ridge

Oak Hill

Mummasburg Road

Carlisle Road

Harrisburg Road

Barlow's Knoll

Gettysburg & Hanover RR

Unfinished RR

Chambersburg Pike

MacPherson Ridge

Oak Ridge

York Road

Lutheran Seminary

Gettysburg

Hanover Road

Fairfield/Hagerstown Road

Seminary Ridge

Benner's Hill

Cemetery Hill

Culp's Hill

Wolf's Hill

Willoughby Run

Emmitsburg Road

Spangler's Spring

Pitzer's Run

Cemetery Ridge

Baltimore Pike

Power's Hill

Peach Orchard

Rock Creek

Wheatfield

Rose Woods

Devil's Den

Little Round Top

Round Top

Taneytown Road

Plum Run

N
W   E
S

0   .5   1
MILES

In the early morning hours of June 28, 1863, in the vicinity of Frederick, Maryland, Major General George Gordon Meade, commanding the V Corps of the Army of the Potomac, was awakened by Colonel James A. Hardie. Meade was handed an order dismissing Major General Joseph Hooker from command of that army and replacing him with Meade. The astonished Meade roused himself, dressed and met with Hooker, who briefed him on the status of the army before taking leave of it. With this change of command, new challenges were created for the Federal army. Dissatisfied with Hooker's performance and failure to impede the Confederate army's incursion into Maryland and Pennsylvania, President Abraham Lincoln relieved him of command. Changing army commanders in mid campaign is a risky venture at any time, but in the current emergency, Lincoln needed a man who could stop Robert E. Lee and his Army of Northern Virginia. Meade was the latest in a string of generals Lincoln turned to for this purpose. Meade was charged with the dual responsibility of safeguarding the National Capital at Washington D.C. as well as giving battle to Robert E. Lee should the latter threaten Philadelphia or Baltimore. Thrust into the command in a campaign already underway gave the irascible Meade little time to make grand strategy. He was forced to react to the Confederate incursion into Pennsylvania, already in progress for the past fortnight, stop that army's progress and inure himself to army command. It is to Meade's credit that he immediately thrust himself into this role, despite the almost impossible task he was given. Lieutenant Frank Haskell, of General John Gibbons' staff, commented that the army, "both officers and men, had no confidence in Hooker." Few soldiers in the army paid much heed to the change in commanders. Franklin Sawyer, of the 8th Ohio Volunteer Infantry, recorded that this change "hardly elicited a comment among the men; the pending battle was the paramount theme of thought and speech."

Confederate General Robert E. Lee began the campaign on June 3, invading Maryland and Pennsylvania on a raid designed to seize supplies, wagons and horses for the Confederate war effort. This foray into northern territory was intended to alleviate the strain of war on Virginia farmlands as well as to foster an increasing discontent with the war in the North—a strike designed both to strengthen Confederate capacity to wage the war while eroding the Northern populace's will to continue to pay the cost of restoring the Union. A victory on Northern soil, might, at last, bring about the ever elusive intervention of Britain and France on the side of the Confederate States of America. Lee took pains to order that his army conduct itself in an orderly fashion, requiring the men to refrain from the taking or destroying of private property. Goods seized were to be paid for with Confederate currency or vouchers. Crossing the Potomac River on June 22, Lee entered Maryland and Pennsylvania.

The appearance of Lee's army in the northern heartland of Pennsylvania created a stir. Local militia was called out, but faced with little formal opposition, Lee directed his army to capture Harrisburg and threaten Baltimore. It was important to seize a victory before the Army of the Potomac could intercede.

Lee learned of the change in Union commanders belatedly. He had his own woes to ponder as he made his way largely unaided by his cavalry. Lee was groping his way toward Gettysburg without his most trusted cavalier, James Ewell Brown (Jeb) Stuart, who was off on a raid designed to screen the main army. Stuart had battled Federal cavalry at Brandy Station on June 9, Aldie on June 17,

Southern infantryman on the march

Middleburg on the 19th and Upperville on the 21st and Hanover on June 30. Stuart was delayed by the newly aggressive Union cavalry and his failure to return to Lee's main army was becoming a concern to the commanding general. The corps and divisions of Lee's army were scattered in the vicinity of Harrisburg, Chambersburg and Carlisle. As resistance crystallized around him, Lee needed to decide which way to strike. Unaided by his cavalry, he was forced to make his decisions with less information than he was used to. Learning that he had drawn the Army of the Potomac in pursuit, he decided to bring his own army together.

The most convenient place for this re-concentration of the Army of Northern Virginia was the town of Gettysburg, a small crossroads

Lieutenant Philip E. Fisher, Co A, 12th Illinois Volunteer Cavalry. Four companies of the 12th Illinois Cavalry fought on McPherson's Ridge on July 1.

Union cavalry scouting a ford

Robert E. Lee courtesy Library of Congress

village of about 2,400 people situated in Adams County, a farm community in the rolling hills of southeastern Pennsylvania. Gettysburg was both strategically and geographically important because it was the nexus of several major roads as well as the terminus of the Gettysburg Railroad, which ran to Hanover. The disparate forces of Lee's army could most readily meet there.

Neither commander had planned for a battle at Gettysburg, but neither could control the sequence of events already in motion. As the two armies marched along the dusty Pennsylvania roads, Meade learned from his cavalry that elements of the Army of Northern Virginia were in the vicinity of Gettysburg. As the two armies wound their respective ways to Gettysburg, the Pennsylvania countryside came alive to combat the Confederate forces raiding their native state.

Harrisburg was threatened. Chambersburg, Cashtown, Emmitsburg and other towns bore witness to the invaders with skirmishing breaking out frequently. Peter W. Alexander, a Confederate correspondent, wrote that "the people along the line of march are overwhelmed with grief and surprise…they remind one of a flock of sheep terrified and bewildered by the howl of the wolf, and are astonished and slavishly thankful that we do not murder, burn and ravage as we go…" Lieutenant William C. Nelson, of the 17th Mississippi Infantry, wrote honestly that "I must confess that the temptation was almost irresistable to do a little destruction, while in Pennsylvania." In addition to the purchase and seizure of supplies and horses, Confederate agents also seized as many Negroes as they could find and sent them south under guard. "They took all they could find," wrote Jemima Cree, of Franklin, "even little children, whom they had to carry on horseback before them."

The state militia was called out, literally in defense of their homes and harassed the Confederate invaders with bushwhacking tactics. In fact, Confederate probes toward Gettysburg encountered such forces and, despite seeing Union cavalry on June 30, they were expecting little serious opposition on July 1 when they returned in force.

Meade reacted to the Confederate presence by moving the Army of the Potomac northward from Frederick, Maryland. The Army of the Potomac was spread over a twenty-five mile front, seeking out the Confederate Army and reacting to reports of local incursions. By the end of June, as Meade scrambled to bring the Army of the Potomac together, he sought suitable ground for

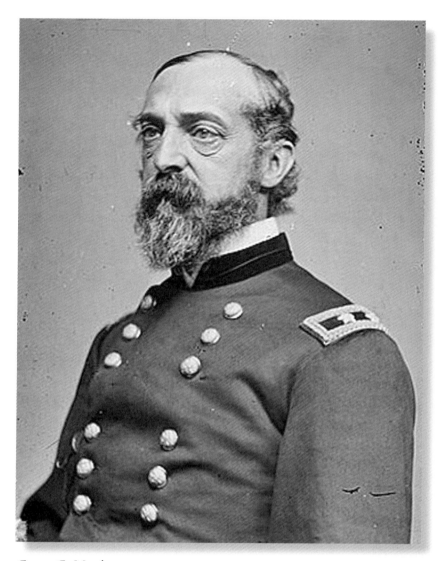

George G. Meade courtesy Library of Congress

a defensive position, resulting in an order late on June 30 to his corps commanders to gather along Pipe Creek, thereby placing the army between where Lee was known to be and Baltimore. As Meade gave orders to consolidate his army, its scattered elements were compelled to make a series of forced marches to bring the whole together. "The men…were not inured to marching," wrote George G. Benedict, of the 12th Vermont, "but they marched well. With sore and blistered and often bleeding feet…they pushed along and made their twenty miles, or nearly that, a day."

For example, the 10th New York Volunteer Infantry was a four company battalion assigned to provost duty. They marched the thirty-three miles from Monocacy Bridge to Uniontown between 10:00 a.m. on June 29 until the early morning hours of the 30th, trying to prod the weary stragglers from the main column to keep up and make their way to the front. The battalion was under the command of Major George F. Hopper and was assigned to provost guard duty in the 3rd Division, II Corps, under the command of Alexander Hays in the brigade commanded by Colonel Thomas A. Smyth. Such an assignment was only given to proven units that were distinguished for their good discipline.

Federal fifes and drums

During the march, the veterans took advantage of the opportunity to equip themselves with much of the cast off items of the new recruits making their first sustained march. Thus, the battalion found itself lavishly equipped with new collars and smoking caps in addition to various other items as it chased the numerous stragglers all along the route. After a rest on June 30, their march to Gettysburg resumed. The pace of the men quickened as the sounds of battle reached them from the distance. The 10th kept its position in rear of the division, policing stragglers, and breaking up impromptu picnics and coffee boiling parties. The footsore and weary battalion reached Gettysburg and went into bivouac at nightfall on July 1, but not before arresting a farmer who refused to provide water from his well to the dehydrated Federal soldiers.

Another Union regiment, The 154th New York, called the Hardtack Regiment, was assigned to the first brigade, second division of the XI Corps. The unit was still understrength after the disastrous defeat suffered at Chancellorsville in May, where it lost 281 out of 590 men engaged. Now the regiment could only muster 274 men present for duty. Colonel Charles R. Coster, formerly of the 154th New York, commanded the undermanned brigade, consisting of the 134th New York, 154th New York and 27th and 73rd Pennsylvania. When the Army of the Potomac began its long trek in response to Robert E. Lee's raid into Maryland and Pennsylvania, the 154th New York, led by the twenty-four year old Lieutenant Colonel Daniel B. Allen, pursued northward making a series of forced marches as it made its way out of Virginia, through Maryland and into Pennsylvania. The pursuit was grueling; often the men marched twenty miles per day through the early summer heat, choking on the clouds of dust kicked up by the trampling of thousands of weary feet. "Oh, how hot it was," lamented one soldier, "no air stirring and the dust about two or three inches deep." At Emmitsburg, early on the morning of July 1, they abandoned their knapsacks and baggage and continued on to Gettysburg in light marching order, minus a detachment of fifty men sent on a reconnaissance.

Sergeant Wyman White, of the 2nd U.S. Sharpshooters, remembered the grueling march. "We had rain in the morning and the roads were muddy and rough. The soldiers kept asking every citizen we met if we had crossed the state line and if we were in Pennsylvania. Sergeant Reynolds…gave the person that said we were in Pennsylvania this answer. "G—D--- your Pennsylvania. The Rebels ought to destroy the whole state if you can't afford better roads. This road is worse than Virginia roads."

The Confederates endured grueling marches too. John C. West, of the 4th Texas Infantry, Hood's Division, wrote to his wife, "We have marched in heat until stalwart men…have fallen dead by the roadside. We have crossed and re-crossed streams, waist deep, with water cold and chilling. We have passed four or five nights and days without changing clothes, which were soaking wet during the entire time…"

Similar stories of the hardship of the long marches in the days immediately preceding the battle abound on both sides. Despite the difficulty the men of both armies persevered, many not knowing their destination—only its ultimate aim; find and destroy the enemy. Avery Harris of the 143rd Pennsylvania Volunteers recalled, "The most we knew in regard to our objective was that Lee was footloose with his Army of Northern Virginia at his heels and ahead of us or on our left flank and we were hurrying forward to get near enough to him to step upon the tail of his army and make him turn around…"

At his point in the war, many regiments and brigades still had their own bands which played stirring airs to keep up the men's spirits on the march. According to one Confederate, "The bands headed each brigade, and played National airs as the troops marched by. Barksdale had a magnificent brass band, while Kershaw had only a fife corps…The music of the fife and drum…gives out more inspiring strains for the marching soldier than any brass band." Union General David B. Birney, commanding the first division of the III Corps, maintained the spirit in his division by having the bands play as the troops marched through towns on the line of march. "By this means the men kept precise step, and besides making an imposing appearance…it prevented the men from straggling, as they became imbued with the pride of making a soldierly display."

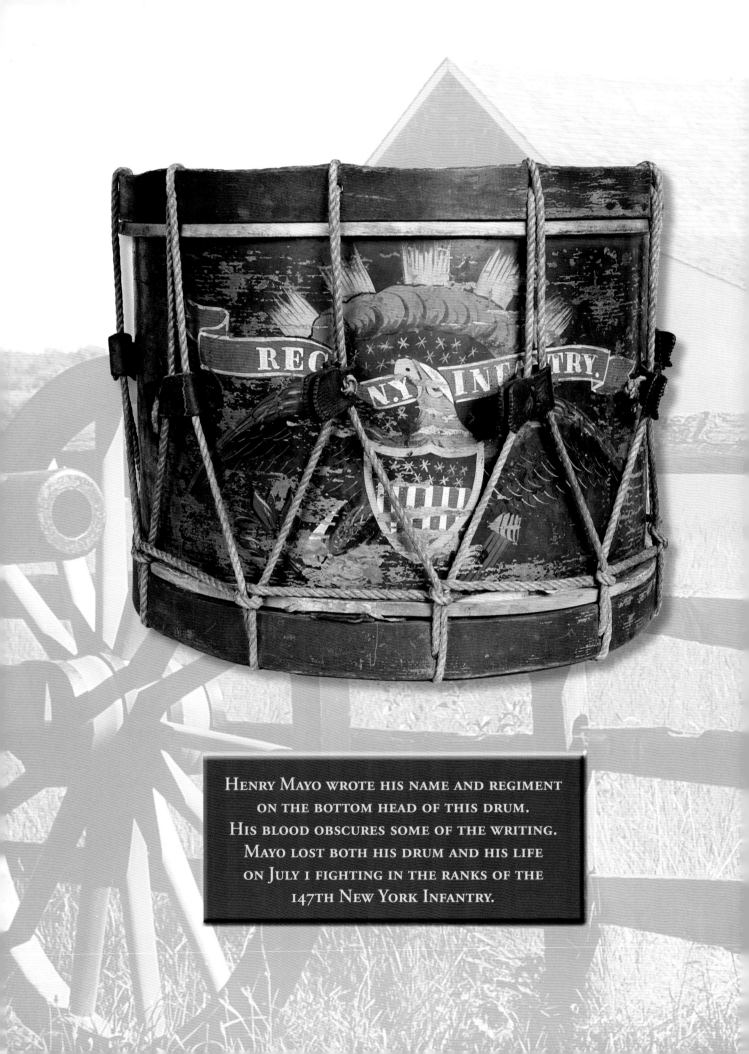

REGT. N.Y. INFANTRY.

HENRY MAYO WROTE HIS NAME AND REGIMENT
ON THE BOTTOM HEAD OF THIS DRUM.
HIS BLOOD OBSCURES SOME OF THE WRITING.
MAYO LOST BOTH HIS DRUM AND HIS LIFE
ON JULY 1 FIGHTING IN THE RANKS OF THE
147TH NEW YORK INFANTRY.

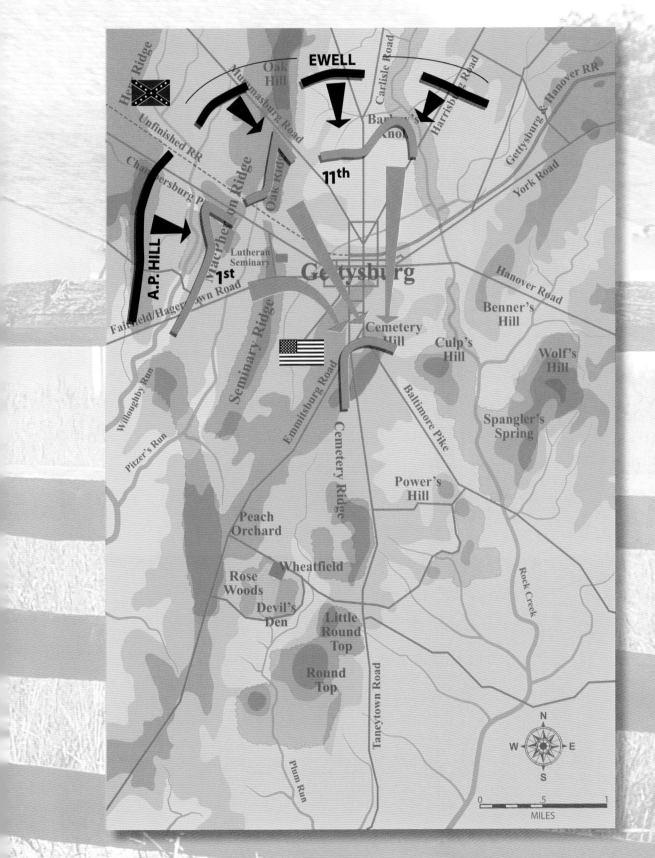

Major General John Buford, commanding the Union cavalry forces in and around Gettysburg on June 30, was aware of the massing Confederate threat. He warned his subordinates that they were protecting a vital objective. The Confederates would "strain every nerve" attempting to take the town, he warned, and the Federals would "have to fight like the devil until supports arrive," if they were to hold it. Buford's cavalry were detailed on the hills and ridges guarding the approaches to the town. In the last days of June, Federal cavalrymen skirmished with elements of the vanguard of Lee's army. Buford was fully aware that the Confederates were coming in force.

In the early morning hours of July 1, vedettes of the 8th Illinois Cavalry of Colonel William Gamble's Brigade and the 9th New York Cavalry,

Confederate corporal

of Colonel Thomas Devin's Brigade, stationed along the ridges overlooking Willoughby Run, spied Confederate forces of Major General Henry Heth's Division moving towards Gettysburg along the Cashtown Pike. A Federal outpost of forty men was posted on Knoxlyn Ridge, along the Cashtown Pike where a stone bridge crossed Marsh Creek in the vicinity of a blacksmith shop. In the early morning light, at about 6:00 a.m., Privates Thomas B. Kelley and James O. Hale, of the 8th Illinois Cavalry, saw a cloud of dust raised up in the distance. They notified their commander, Lieutenant Marcellus Jones, who was in camp some 300 yards to the rear. Keeping watch on the growing dust cloud in the increasing light, it soon was apparent that the Confederate army was approaching. Jones sent a dispatch up the chain of command and monitored the approaching column. Lieutenant Jones borrowed a Spencer carbine from Sergeant Levi Shafer, rested the gun along the top rail of a fence, and fired a shot at the approaching enemy column. He missed! The battle of Gettysburg had begun.

The Confederates, Alabama infantry from Brigadier General James Jay Archer's Brigade of Henry Heth's Division, were advancing towards Gettysburg along the Cashtown Pike. Taking note of the force posted on the ridge, the Confederates deployed a skirmish line, two companies of the 13th Alabama and the 5th Alabama Battalion, before resuming the advance towards town with the intention of driving the opposition away.

Lietenant Colonel S. G. Shepard, of the Seventh Tennessee Infantry briefly described the Confederate advance towards the thin Federal cavalry line. "We left our camp near Cashtown, Pa., early on the morning of July 1, and marched down the turnpike road leading to Gettysburg. We had advanced about 3 miles when we came upon the enemy's pickets, who gradually fell back before us for about 3 miles, which brought us in sight of the enemy, upon a slight eminence in our front and to the right of the road. General Archer halted for a short time while a section of a battery opened fire upon them. He then deployed the brigade in line, and advanced directly upon the enemy through an open field."

As the cavalry forces under John Buford prepared to receive the Confederate attack along McPherson's Ridge, riders were sent to alert Union infantry forces en route to Gettysburg that Confederate infantry was advancing upon the town in force. Major General John F. Reynolds, commanding the I Corps, came forward to reconnoiter the ground and meet with Buford, who was observing the battle from the cupola of the Lutheran Seminary. Both generals immediately recognized the importance of haste if they were to hold the position and keep possession of the crossroads. In an impromptu council of war, they decided to hold the favorable high ground on the ridges until the main army under Meade could arrive. Reynolds gave orders hastening his I Corps forward. The XI Corps, under Major General Oliver O. Howard, was also ordered to hasten to the field. The Battle of Gettysburg was a meeting engagement. As the two armies collided unexpectedly,

The forage cap of 8th Illinois Calvary Corporal Levi Shafer, whose carbine fired the battle's first shot. Levi carved his initials 'LS' into the brim's underside.

elements of both armies were forced into action immediately upon their arrival. The course of the battle ebbed and flowed according to fortune and the arrival of new strength.

On the Confederate side, Robert E. Lee did not want to bring on a general engagement, but quickened the march of his forces towards the crossroads. The Confederate army was scattered to the east and north of the town. Converging roads would reunite them at Gettysburg. Heth's Division of A.P. Hill's Corps was deploying for battle to seize the town. The other Confederate forces approaching town from the north and east and would arrive in a timely fashion and in ideal position to adapt to Heth's deployment.

All morning the skirmishing between Buford's cavalry and Heth's advance units continued and intensified. The Union cavalry delayed the advance of the Confederate infantrymen for several hours, forcing them to halt and deploy into line of battle once they realized the cavalry was too strong to be brushed aside with just a skirmish line. Giving ground grudgingly, the horse soldiers fell back from ridge to ridge, buying time and delaying the Confederate advance until the Union foot soldiers could deploy.

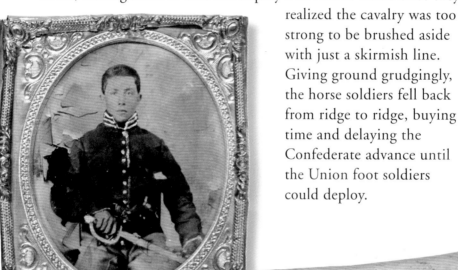

Tintype and bugle of Private Morgan Hughes, bugler of Co E, 8th Illinois Cavalry. The 8th Illinois is widely credited with firing the first shot of the battle.

Generals John Buford and John Reynolds confer on the battlefield. "The Devil's to pay,"
Buford exclaimed as they viewed the Confederate advance.

Private Henry McCollum, Co. H 2nd Wisconsin Infantry was killed in action near McPherson's Woods on July 1.

"The Chosen Ground" depicts I Corps commander Major General John Reynolds leading the 2nd Wisconsin of the Iron Brigade into the battle on July 1.

Reynolds was personally directing the positioning of his Corps. "Forward men, forward, for God's sake, and drive those fellows out of the woods," Reynolds commanded. Scarcely had Reynolds rode up when a Confederate rifleman felled him with a fatal wound to the head. The dying Reynolds never knew what struck him. The I Corps went into the fight without its beloved commander. Major General Abner Doubleday, senior division commander, assumed command of the I Corps upon Reynolds' death. The loss of Reynolds was a severe blow as he was "one of the *soldier* Generals of the army…"

Brigadier General Lysander Cutler's Brigade was the vanguard of the I Corps as it neared Gettysburg. Led by Colonel Edward B. Fowler, the 14th Brooklyn trailed the second brigade as it trudged along the Chambersburg Road. Clad in their flashy chasseur style uniforms, with blue cap and coat with red trimmings, and red pants, this hard-fighting unit had earned the name "Red-legged devils" from begrudging yet admiring Confederate combatants. The roar of artillery, interspersed with small arms fire, told one and all that there would be "serious work ahead" en route to McPherson's Woods, where Buford's cavalry was engaged with Confederate infantry. As the regiment went into line along the Chambersburg Road, it began to take heavy fire. It was while they were deploying into line that General Reynolds was killed. Men of the 14th Brooklyn carried him from the field. The battle for the woods raged in their front when they began taking additional fire from the flank and rear. The regiment was ordered to drop its packs and double quick march into action.

Once the Confederates were in line they advanced, making their way through woods. An advance in force was meant to test the strength of Federal resistance. The first test of the strength of the Union line came as the I

Major Hezakiah Allen, Co. H, 13th Alabama Infantry, Archer's Brigade, Heth's Division fought in the opening stages of the battle on July 1. On July 3, they planted their flag on the Union works on Cemetery Ridge before being driven back.

Corps arrived on the field to relieve Buford's beleaguered cavalrymen. Among the first troops of the I Corps to go into battle were the black-hatted veterans of the Iron Brigade, First Brigade of James Wadsworth's First Division. As the embattled Confederates advanced, sensing a final victory over the withdrawing cavalry, they were met by a volley of musketry. Recognizing the black hats of the Iron Brigade, the Rebels knew they were in for a hot, stand up fight, no longer just a skirmish with stubborn dismounted cavalry.

Archer's and Davis' brigades of Heth's Division assaulted Cutler's men as they went into action, forcing them to fall back. The Iron Brigade arrived in time to crash into Archer's Brigade, driving him back. Confederate Gen. J.R. Davis' Mississippi Brigade was advancing through a railroad cut and firing upon Cutler's men. The 14th Brooklyn, joining with the 6th Wisconsin of the Iron Brigade and the 95th New York, changed front and stormed the railroad cut, outflanking the trapped Southerners and raking them with a galling fire. This move resulted in the capture of hundreds of Davis' Mississippians, who "fought with the ferocity of wildcats." The 6th Wisconsin took heavy casualties, but in the ferocious fighting wrested away the colors of the 2nd Mississippi as a trophy of the battle. (Later, the 14th Brooklyn fought with distinction at Culp's Hill, on July 2nd and 3rd, and were credited with saving the Union position on that important hilltop). The

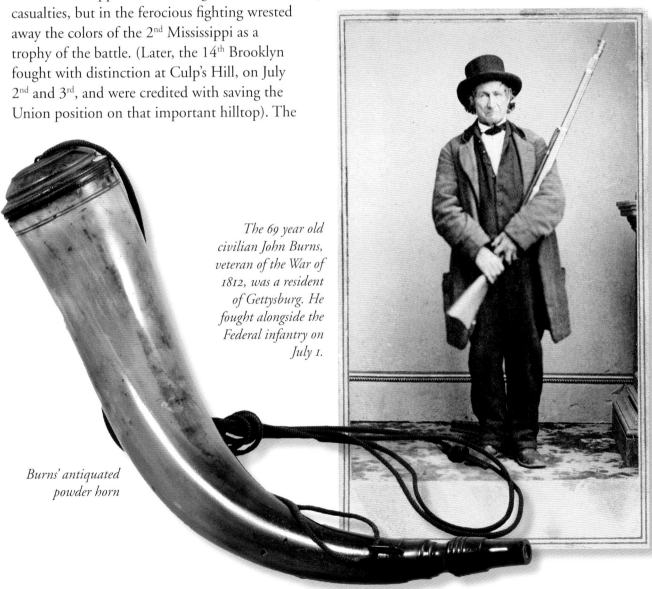

The 69 year old civilian John Burns, veteran of the War of 1812, was a resident of Gettysburg. He fought alongside the Federal infantry on July 1.

Burns' antiquated powder horn

Federals fell back to solidify their line. John Burns, a 69 year old civilian resident of the town and a veteran of the War of 1812, fell in and fought along with the boys in blue, determined to make a stand for his home, and securing for himself a place in the lore of the battle.

Late in the morning of July 1, Colonel Roy Stone's Bucktail Brigade took position along the Chambersburg Pike at the McPherson Farm and took a brief respite while watching the battle near the railroad cut from a distance. Stray artillery shells burst in their vicinity, but it was not until one o'clock p.m. when Robert E. Rodes' Division of Major General Richard S. Ewell's Corps appeared that they became seriously engaged. As they began to take enfilading fire from Rodes' artillery stationed atop Oak Hill, the Pennsylvanians formed along the Chambersburg Pike. This move placed them under a crossfire from artillery on Herr Ridge. Taking heavy casualties, the Bucktails engaged

The Unfinished Railroad Cut proved to be a trap for many Confederates.

in long range musketry against the Confederate battlelines that were developing to their north and west. Rodes advanced and engaged the Bucktails at the railroad cut. Once again the fighting in this area was savage. Superior numbers won out over valor and the Federals retreated.

John Bodler, of the 149th Pennsylvania, recalled, "Ran double quick 3 miles. The battle commenced shortly after our arrival. Our Brigade had to go straightway into the fire…One bomb exploded 4 feet away from me. My horse got a piece of it in the head. Our Division had heavy loss, almost all officers died. We had to draw back a mile further." "No language," reported Colonel Roy Stone, "can do justice to the conduct of my officers and men on the bloody first day, to the coolness with which they watched and awaited under a fierce storm of shot and shell, the approach of the enemy's overwhelming masses, to their ready obedience to orders, and prompt and perfect execution, under fire, of all the tactic of the battle-field, to the fierceness of their repeated attacks, and to the desperate tenacity of their resistance. They fought as though each man felt that upon his own arm hung the fate of the day and the nation. Nearly two-thirds of my command fell on the field. Every field officer, save one, was wounded and disabled."

The Model 1858 U.S. Regulation Hardee Hat with ostrich plume was the signature headgear of the Iron Brigade.

6th Wisconsin Infantryman in campaign dress.

As the battle progressed, the XI Corps arrived and went into line and was engaged by the Confederate attack. Now, the sustained onslaught by the superior numbers of Rodes, Pender, Early and Heth told. The XI Corps made a brief stand, but ultimately was overrun and forced to retreat. This uncovered the I Corps which also gave way. During this fighting, Lieutenant Bayard Wilkeson of Battery G, 4th U. S. Artillery, was severely wounded as he served his guns on the Union right flank. The youth's right leg had been nearly torn away by an exploding shell. As his men fled, Wilkeson amputated his own leg with a pocket knife, using his sash as a tourniquet. The boy lieutenant later died from his wounds. Today, his kepi, sash and commission are on display in the Gettysburg Museum.

Confederate artillery officer's frock coat.

The 154th New York, assigned to Colonel Charles Coster's Brigade of Von Steinwehr's Division, traveled through rain and mud all morning until reaching the hills near Gettysburg, where the unmistakable sounds of battle fell upon their ears. Orders came to make haste to Gettysburg, adding urgency to the last leg of the march. Upon arriving, the regiment crossed the open fields near the Codori Farm and took position in Evergreen Cemetery, on Cemetery Hill, south of town. Finally the men rested, had a hasty meal and filled their canteens. From this vantage point they witnessed the progress of the battle as it unfolded to the north, and observed the collapse of the XI Corps as it succumbed to the Southern onslaught of Jubal Early's Division.

All too soon orders came to reinforce the right flank of Francis Barlow's Division and cover the retreat of the beaten first and third divisions of the XI Corps. The brigade hurriedly made its way through the streets of Gettysburg, which were lined with wounded and stragglers from the battle. Double-quicking through "the confusion and disaster" in town, the brigade made its way up Stratton Street into the Kuhn Brickyard east of the Harrisburg Road. Here the 154th New York went into

The 14th Brooklyn advancing across the Chambersburg Pike.

Confederate artilleryman's trousers with red stripes.

This Confederate pouch held friction primers used to ignite the powder charge in the cannon's barrel. A similar version can be seen below the arm of the nearest artilleryman in the painting above.

Bucktail Private Lorenzo J. Curtis Co D, 143rd Pennsylvania. The Bucktails fought at Reynolds Grove and the Railroad Cut before falling back with the I Corps.

line along the rail fences in the brickyard, in front of the kilns, holding the center of the line between the 134th New York on the left and the 27th Pennsylvania on the right, with the 73rd Pennsylvania in reserve. The hastily chosen position was unfortunate as the wheat fields in front were elevated, thereby shielding the advance of the Confederates and rendering the defenders' position vulnerable with a limited field of fire. The New Yorkers were directed to kneel and not to fire until "the enemy were close enough to make our volley effective."

Then seemingly innumerable battle flags of the Confederates suddenly appeared on the ground above the brickyard. Two full brigades of southerners were attacking across a front that overlapped both flanks of the defenders. The battle could have only one outcome, despite the furious stand made by the New Yorkers and Pennsylvanians of Coster's Brigade, who fired nine volleys at the attackers before being overrun. The collapse of this position, before an orderly retreat could be conducted, resulted in a full scale rout in which most of the survivors were captured. Some companies never received word to retreat and were captured after a last ditch hand to hand struggle in front of the kilns. The remnants of the brigade fled into Gettysburg in disorder, pursued by the victorious Southerners.

No official report of the action made its way into the *Official Records.* Losses for the 154th New York at Gettysburg show six enlisted men killed, five mortally wounded, three officers and twenty-six men wounded and eleven officers and 161 enlisted men missing or captured. Sixty of those captured would die in prison camps.

Today the 154th New York State Infantry is not forgotten at Gettysburg.
An eighty foot mural depicting the fight in the brickyard adorns the
wall a few feet behind the monument to the Hardtack Regiment
on Coster Avenue. A stone tablet chronicling the Humiston story is
located a short distance to the south of Coster Avenue.

The collapse of the Union line resulted in a flood of refugees into
the streets of Gettysburg. Men ran, according to Frank Haskell, "in
houses, in barns, in yards and cellars, throwing away their arms,
they sought to hide like rabbits…" Many were captured.
Some of the more fortunate, like Brigadier General
Alexander Schimmelfennig, were able to evade
the pursuit of the victorious Confederates by
hiding in the town.

*The bucktail, cap box,
epaulettes and bullseye
canteen of John Bodler, 149th
Pennsylvania Volunteers, of the
Bucktail Brigade.*

The battle also left its marks upon the town. Businesses, like W.T. King's tailor shop, and homes were riddled with bullets. Some still show the scars today. Civilians were not immune to the effects of the battle. Some hid or fled, some like John Burns took active part. Others helped the wounded or hid refugees. Jennie Wade, a twenty year old woman, was shot by an errant bullet as she was baking bread in her sister's kitchen. She was the only known civilian killed in the battle.

This Confederate plug hat is typical of the civilian type headgear favored by the Southern forces.

Upon his arrival at Gettysburg, XI Corps commander Major General Oliver O. Howard established his headquarters on the high ground of Cemetery Ridge, near the cemetery itself. Here he fashioned a line with his artillery and reserves as two of his divisions went into battle, marching through the town trying to establish a connection on the right of the hard-pressed I Corps. Rather than committing his entire corps, Howard held one division (Steinwehr's) in reserve on Cemetery Ridge. It was to this line that the remnants of the two defeated Union Corps rallied.

Major General Winfield S. Hancock arrived on the field, empowered by Meade to take command. He consulted with Howard and then began making his dispositions. As additional Union corps arrived on the field they were sent to reinforce the line established by Hancock. The Union forces positioned themselves during the rest of the day and night and by mid-morning of July 2 were in place. The shattered remnants of the I and XI Corps held Cemetery Hill and the western slope of Culp's Hill, which was occupied in force by the XII Corps. Hancock's II Corps extended along Cemetery Hill to Cemetery Ridge, beyond which the III Corps extended the line to the left all the way to Little Round Top. The V Corps was held in reserve between the Taneytown and Baltimore roads. The VI Corps had not yet arrived but was marching through the night. Hancock and Meade determined to hold the high ground and await Confederate attacks. Union troops on East Cemetery Hill and Culp's Hill busied themselves through the night building field fortifications.

Lee, for his part, was determined to strike a telling blow. After the Federals were driven from Seminary Ridge, the Confederate attack stalled. A.P. Hill's Corps had borne the brunt of the fighting and could not continue the attack. General Richard S. Ewell and his corps were given discretionary orders by Lee to take Cemetery Hill if practicable, but Ewell demurred, feeling his men needed to rest. Fighting for the day had ended. Lee decided to stay and fight, intending to strike hard at both Union flanks on July 2 while keeping the troops in the center tied down, preventing them from

The Bible of William E. Ventress, fifer, Co. A, 5ᵗʰ Alabama Infantry. Inscribed within Ventress requested that the finder send the bible to his wife.

This .58 caliber black leather cartridge box marked AH Odell, 5ᵗʰ Alabama Infantry, was found on the Gettysburg battlefield.

reinforcing the threatened flanks. Somewhere, in Lee's estimation, the Union line would falter and the successes of July 1 could be exploited into a decisive victory.

Thomas L. Livermore, commanding the ambulance corps of the II Corps rode into the cemetery on the evening of July 1 and observed, "this was the second graveyard in which our armies had contended in battles in which I was…I saw dead men and horses lying among graves. I do not know of a stranger thing in the war than these contentions over the heads of the dead who died in peace and the expectation of having their bones lie in that most peaceful solitude which civilization permits."

Federal soldier W.T. King and his bullet-riddled Gettysburg shop sign.
courtesy of Adams County Historical Society

The young Jennie Wade was the sole civilian casualty.
courtesy of Adams County Historical Society

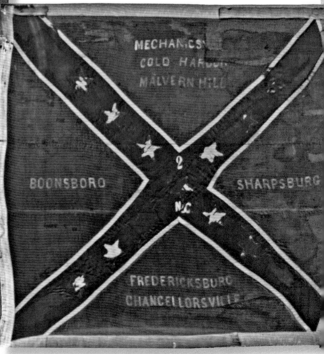

Battleflag of the 2nd North Carolina Infantry.

The Codori House and meat market at 44 York Street at the time of the battle.

THE CHILDREN OF THE BATTLEFIELD

The fate of one man listed as missing is one of the more poignant episodes of the battle, if not the war. The body of Sergeant Amos Humiston, Co. C, 154th New York was discovered in town after the battle. The corpse was without identification, but when the burial squad discovered him, they found an ambrotype photo of three young children clutched in his hand. The heartrending tale of a dying father's last gaze of his three children caused a nationwide sensation. Through the efforts of Dr. John F. Bournes, of Philadelphia, numerous copies of the photograph were circulated and reprinted in Northern newspapers nationwide. Finally, the aggrieved widow, Phylinda Humiston, came forward after seeing the photo. She identified her dead husband, and the photo of their three children, Franklin, Frederick and Alice. The story of the dying father and the search for his identity tugged at the heartstrings of the nation. A poem "*The Children of the Battlefield,*" was written and set to music. At Gettysburg, the Soldiers' Orphans' Home was founded in 1866 to care for the orphans of battle. Phylinda Humiston was one of the first matrons of this orphanage, directed by Dr. Bournes and lived there with her three children until 1869 when she remarried and moved away. Amos Humiston lies in the New York section of the National Cemetery.

"THE SOLDIER'S CHILDREN"
(see other side)

SERGT. AMOS HUMISTON,
Of the 154th N. Y. Vols.

"The Children of the Battlefield", Frank, Alice and Freddie Humiston and a carte-de-visite of their fallen father.

Sergeant Amos Humiston, Co C., 154th New York Infantry, the Hardtack Regiment.

THIS CONFEDERATE
1ST SERGEANT'S SHELL JACKET,
WITH BLUE RANK STRIPES,
WAS RECOVERED FROM THE
GETTYSBURG BATTLEFIELD.

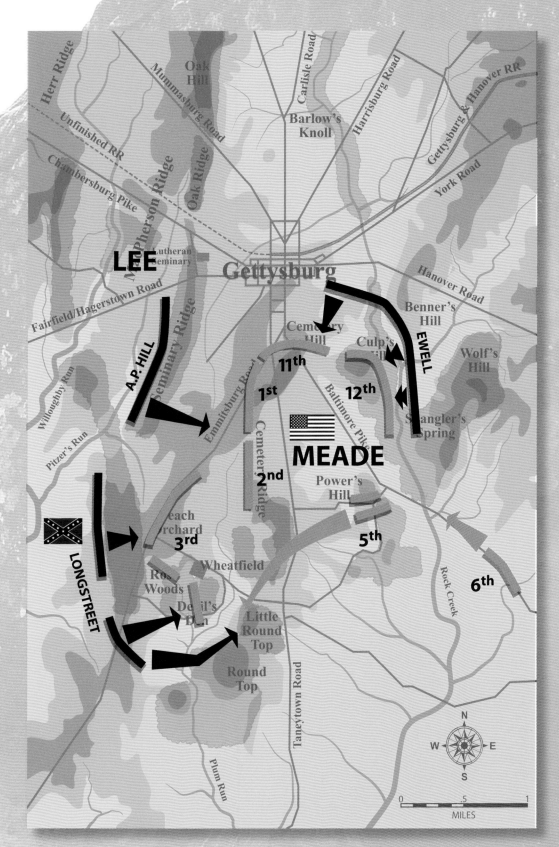

JULY 2

J uly 2 was a day never to be forgotten by those who endured it. Starting out as peaceably as two armies in battle can be, the day would prove to be one of the bloodiest of the war, with fierce combat waging on both flanks and in the center. The confused fighting kept both armies on edge throughout the day. Victory and defeat were decided only by the narrowest of margins. It would be a day of unlikely heroics, timely intervention and missed opportunities.

Meade had concentrated on stabilizing his line along the heights, taking best advantage of the terrain. The Union line had been fashioned during the night into the so called fishhook shaped line from Culp's Hill to the Round Tops. All but the VI Corps were present on the battlefield. The V Corps which had come up during the night

Lieutenant General James Longstreet, senior Confederate corps comman

Major General Daniel Sickles,
Commander of III Corps.
courtesy Library of Congress

Confederate Reconnaissance

was held in reserve. As the day progressed, Major General Daniel Sickles, commanding the III Corps, saw enemy activity in his front and felt that his line was endangered. When his advancing sharpshooters were engaged by Confederate skirmishers posted in Pitzer's Woods, Sickles took it upon himself to advance his entire corps forward to the west, about three quarters of a mile, to take advantage of an elevation that would give him command of the Emmitsburg Road.

Without notifying Meade, Sickles abandoned his assigned position, leaving a substantial gap of 500 yards in the Federal line. Sickles' new line extended from the rocky area known as Devil's Den to the

A model 1861 forage cap with red cloth diamond, depicting 1st Division, III Corps, was worn by John Unger, Co B, 40th New York Volunteers.

This present day photo marks the apex of Sickle's III Corps salient in the Peach Orchard.

elevated ground of the Sherfy Peach Orchard and thence north along the Emmitsburg Road for nearly a mile. The move exposed both of Sickles' flanks and uncovered Hancock's left flank on Cemetery Ridge, leaving Little Round Top, the key to the Union line, uncovered and vulnerable to attack. Sickles' high ground commanded the Emmitsburg Road, but placed him directly in harm's way.

Meade learned of Sickles' maverick move only after the fact. As he reconnoitered the line, Meade was incensed when he discovered the change of position. Seeing increased Confederate activity, which clearly indicated an attack, Meade could not order Sickles to return to the original line. Instead, Meade sent orders to the V Corps under Major General George Sykes, to move up in support of Sickles. This movement left only the hard marching and tired VI Corps in reserve. To reinforce Sickles' line, several batteries of artillery were ordered up to the support of the forces at the Peach Orchard. The makeshift line stood well in advance of the main Union line on Cemetery Ridge.

Robert E. Lee had determined to stay at Gettysburg and fight, despite the objections of Lieutenant General James Longstreet, his senior Corps commander. Lee issued orders early in the morning for his army to strike hard at both Union flanks. Scouts were sent out to reconnoiter the Union line and find a vantage point for the attack. The best Confederate information put the Federals in weak strength in the vicinity of the Peach Orchard.

Longstreet intended to use the divisions of John B. Hood, Lafayette McLaws and Richard H. Anderson's division of A.P. Hill's corps. He would turn the Federal left flank while hitting their line along the Emmitsburg Road, the

Isaac Anderson Reed, Co H, 7th Georgia Infantry, of General George T. Anderson's Brigade, guarded the left flank of Hood's Division as it assaulted the Devil's Den.

A Confederate kepi with blue band would under army regulations denote infantry, but by 1863 little adherence to the regulations could be expected from the hard-pressed supply depots of the South.

Peach Orchard and on Cemetery Ridge. "The intention was to get in rear of the enemy," wrote Lafayette McLaws.

Longstreet, who preferred to fight defensively, was opposed to the idea and argued long with Lee against the nature of the attack. He preferred to force the Federals to come to him. All of Longstreet's arguments were nullified by Lee. Finally and reluctantly, Longstreet gave the necessary orders to move his corps across the field. Because he protested Lee's order, Longstreet has received much criticism from history, both for the amount of time it took to marshal his forces and to finally begin the attack. In fairness to him, it must be remembered that many of his troops endured a grueling twenty mile march just to reach the battlefield and Pickett's Division was not even there yet. John West, 4th Texas, recalled, "We marched all night (July 1)…in order to reach the battlefield in time…" Despite his misgivings, Longstreet, after an hours long effort to march his corps to the staging point for the attack, gave the orders to advance for the assault on the Union left, where the III Corps was posted. It was late in the afternoon of July 2 when it finally got underway.

Although Longstreet's attack was long delayed, it was all too soon for the men wearing blue uniforms. No sooner had Meade made arrangements to settle his line and to send support to Sickles than the Confederates struck in force. Beginning in the area of Devil's Den, the attack broke out all along the length of the line extending from Devil's Den to Little Round Top, the Wheatfield and the Peach Orchard salient. As the Confederate artillery

This officer's frock coat belonged to Captain Isaac Nicholls of Co G, 124th New York Infantry, "The Orange Blossoms." Nicholls was killed in action on July 2.

KEITH ROCCO ® '96

*Two Minie
bullets, fused
together by the force of their impact,
recovered from a tree on present day
East Confederate Avenue.*

*Today it stands quaint and idyllic, but
on July 2, the Sherfy House, opposite
the Peach Orchard, witnessed fierce
fighting. The 114th Pennsylvania,
represented by this figure, would lose
heavily in this area, eventually being
enveloped and crushed by the attack of
Barksdale's Brigade.*

opened along the line, the infantry attack went forward. Hood's Division, consisting of Law's, Robertson's, Benning's and Anderson's Brigades, struck the left of Sickles' redeployed line while Lafayette McLaws' Division, consisting of the brigades of Barksdale, Kershaw, Semmes and Wofford advanced against the exposed III Corps near its salient around the Peach Orchard.

In the vicinity of the Devil's Den, John Bell Hood was to spearhead the assault with his division. Hood was on the extreme left with McLaws to his right. Hood protested the attack orders to Longstreet to no avail. He argued that attacking the III Corps head on was foolhardy. The possibility of striking them from the flank and rear existed because of the III Corps' advanced position. Longstreet, after having been overruled himself by Lee, was in no mood to listen to dissent from his own subordinates. The attack would go forward as Lee directed, come what may. Hood then ordered his division forward across some of the roughest terrain on the battlefield. Evander Law's Brigade attacked towards Houck's Ridge and the Devil's Den, flanked by Robertson's Brigade. The attack was subjected to artillery fire from Houck's Ridge and the Peach Orchard every step of the way.

Hood was seriously wounded at the beginning of the attack and command control of the assault was lost. "When the command was given to charge we moved forward as fast as we could…It was between a half and three-quarters of a mile across an open field, over a marshy branch, over a stone fence and up a very rugged and rocky hill…" wrote John West, of the 4th Texas. The ridge was defended by Union men of the III Corps Division of Brigadier General

Confederates, now in control of the Devil's Den, replenish their cartridge boxes and set their sights on the next objective, Little Round Top, seen in the distance.

Custom made .52 caliber 36 pound bench or target rifle. The initials HCP, believed to be Henry Clay Powell, Co K, 1st Texas Infantry are inscribed on a silver set plate in the stock.

J. H. Hobart Ward (2nd Brigade, 1st Division) including the 124th New York, known as the Orange Blossom Regiment. Colonel Ellis and Major James Cromwell of the 124th were mounted despite protests that they would be killed. Major Cromwell stated "The men must see us today."

As the Confederates attacked, the four guns of Capt. James E. Smith's 4th New York Independent Battery fired in support of the defenders, dueling with Confederate artillery on Warfield Ridge. The 3rd Arkansas and 1st Texas Infantry reached the stone wall in the triangular field from which place they sniped at Smith's gunners. The 3rd Arkansas was fought to a standstill by the 20th Indiana and the 86th New York who were supported by fire from the 124th New York. John Wilkerson of the 3rd Arkansas recalled that, "our ranks were getting thin. It was fight all the time. Each side wanted the protection of those rocks…"

Private William A. Fletcher, Co F, 5th Texas Infantry, of Brigadier General Jerome Robertson's Brigade, fought through the Devils Den and attacked Little Round Top.

"Here it was that our brave Colonel and Major were killed and our Lieutenant Colonel wounded. For two and a half hours we held the ground against three times our number. Here, too, we lost a good many men," recalled John W. Pitts. Captain Charles Weygant, of the 124th New York described the aftermath of the attack. "The slope in front was strewn with our dead, and not a few of our severely wounded lay beyond the reach of their unscathed comrades, bleeding, helpless, and some of them dying."

As was occurring elsewhere, the overwhelming tide of Confederates had its inevitable effect. The combined pressure of Law's and Robertson's brigades, backed by Benning's Brigade broke the Union

line on Houck's Ridge. The 124th New York and other units were driven back. Without infantry support, Smith lost all of his guns when Benning's brigade charged headlong into the storm of shot and canister, ignoring casualties that ripped holes in their ranks. "The 15th and 20th (Georgia) clambered over the rocks and pressed forward…the enemy, dismayed at such daring, began to break…"

The victorious Confederates now concentrated on taking the Slaughter Pen and advancing on Little Round Top. Law's and Robertson's brigades attacked Devil's Den and Little Round Top simultaneously. Robertson's 1st Texas and 3rd Arkansas initially attacked Devil's Den. Later, Law's 44th and 48th Alabama regiments joined in the fray. Benning's Brigade added weight to their attacks. As more Confederates engaged, Union reinforcements, including the 40th New York and the 6th New Jersey came up in support to fend off Benning's 2nd and 17th Georgia in the gorge below the big rocks.

Meantime, Law's Brigade, the 4th, 15th and 47th Alabama, supported by Robertson's 4th and 5th Texas, launched their attacks against Little Round Top. As Law's and Benning's Brigades fought through the Devil's Den and Slaughter Pen they made and supported several attacks against Little Round Top. The direct attacks were repulsed. Many of the men of the 4th and 5th Texas (who were repulsed in their attack against Little Round Top) took up firing positions among the ancient boulders in Devil's Den. Here they engaged in long range sniping with the defenders on Little Round Top. Private William Fletcher, of the 5th Texas, participated in the unsuccessful attacks on Little Round Top and retreated back to Devil's Den. "I had no fear of the enemy charging and capturing the retreating forces, for they had ample dead and wounded to satisfy them…"

A Confederate sharpshooter's nest, erected on July 2 in the Devil's Den, remains a part of the battlefield to the present day.

Little Round Top is the name given to a hill that is one of the most widely visited spots on any Civil War battlefield. The rocky knoll, situated to the west of Gettysburg, anchored the left of the Union line along Cemetery Ridge and overlooks the area of some of the fiercest fighting, including the Wheatfield and Devil's Den. Called Little Round Top because it is situated adjacent to a similar, but larger and more heavily wooded knoll, Big Round Top, the hill gained immortality because of what happened, and what didn't happen, on its slopes on the late afternoon of July 2, 1863.

Brigadier General Gouverneur K. Warren, Chief Engineer of the Army of the Potomac, was reconnoitering the Union position at the request of General Meade after learning of Sickles' unauthorized advance. What Warren discovered stunned him. Little Round Top was unmanned except for a small detachment of signalmen. Recognizing that the hill was the key to the entire Union line, Warren immediately sent an aide to get reinforcements. Warren reacted to what he saw—Confederates advancing between the buildings of the Slyder Farm. The meaning of this was unmistakable— the Confederates were massed preparatory to attacking. Without immediate support, Little Round Top would easily fall.

Warren's aide found General George Sykes, commander of the V Corps. Sykes gave orders for a brigade to hasten to Little Round Top. Brigadier General James Barnes, whose division was selected, was

Brigadier General Gouverneur K. War the savior of Little Round Top.
courtesy of Library of Congress

G.K. Warren's field telescope

Brigade commander Strong Vincent, riding crop in hand, indicates positions to Colonel Joshua Chamberlain, ordering him to "Hold the Ground at all Hazards".

THE 140TH NEW YORK INFANTRY, IN THE NICK OF TIME, ENGAGE THE ENEMY ON THE WESTERN SLOPE OF LITTLE ROUND TOP. 19 YEAR OLD LIEUTENANT CHARLES KLINE, SEEN HERE WITH PISTOL IN HAND, WAS WOUNDED IN THE RIGHT THIGH DURING THIS ACTION. AT FIRST THOUGHT TO BE A NON-LIFE THREATENING INJURY, KLINE WOULD DIE AS A RESULT OF THE GUNSHOT ON JULY 19.

The French-Algerian influenced
Zouave uniform of the 146th New
York Infantry who fought alongside the
140th New York on Little Round Top.

not at hand, but Colonel Strong Vincent was, and acting upon his own responsibility, immediately volunteered to take his brigade to the threatened spot. Vincent's men scrambled up the northern slope of Little Round Top to occupy defensive positions in the face of the Confederate advance. Vincent led the brigade, consisting of the 44th New York, 16th Michigan, 83rd Pennsylvania and 20th Maine regiments. The men arranged themselves on the threatened slopes, making use of the natural cover provided by the boulders that jutted out of the sides of the knoll. Colonel Joshua L. Chamberlain,

Model 1861 green wool kepi worn by Berdan's Sharpshooters, displaying the red diamond badge of 1st Division, III Corps.

Sharps New Model 1859 Military Rifle .52 caliber breechloader was used by Co G 1st U.S. Sharp Shooters.

commanding the 20th Maine, on the extreme Union left flank, was ordered to "hold this ground at all hazards."

Warren was grazed in the throat by a musket ball as he continued to direct the placement of units on the hill. Battery D, 5th U.S. Artillery, commanded by Lieutenant Charles Hazlett was manhandled up the slopes of Little Round Top. Warren still needed men and as he rode down from the hill he encountered Brigadier General Stephen H. Weed's Brigade, which he himself had commanded earlier in the war. Warren quieted the cheering men and approached Colonel Patrick O'Rorke, acting as brigade commander. "Paddy, give me a regiment," he implored. Warren overrode O'Rorke's objections, and assumed responsibility for re-directing O'Rorke's men. The 140th New York, hastened off to aid the already beleaguered Union forces on Little Round Top. Warren's quick action sent troops to the summit of Little Round Top just in time to meet the Confederate assault.

On Little Round Top, the Confederate attack was lapping around the Union right flank, where the undermanned 16th Michigan was stationed with the 44th New York to its left. Strong Vincent directed the 140th New York into the maelstrom of the Confederate attack. "Down this way boys," yelled O'Rorke, waving his sword over his head as he led the men down the slope into the Confederates, the 4th and 5th Texas and 48th Alabama. "We went in with a cheer," wrote one soldier, "The Rebels looked at us...then they gave us a murderous volley…Our men fell at every step they took." As Vincent urged on his men, he was mortally wounded. Charging with unloaded rifles, the New Yorkers were able to blunt the Confederate assault, driving back the 48th Alabama and the 4th Texas, thereby solidifying the Union right flank. The emergency here, had passed. The New Yorkers took position behind the rocks and boulders to snipe at Rebels in Devil's Den and the Valley of Death.

The bent back wing of the 20th Maine struggles to hold their position against yet another Confederate attack. Within moments following this scene, Colonel Chamberlain will order a surprise bayonet attack down the hill which will clear the enemy and help save the Federal southern flank.

The 20th Maine Infantry was posted at the extreme left flank of the Union line and ordered to hold the position at all hazards. Colonel Joshua Lawrence Chamberlain, a divinity professor from Bowdoin College in Brunswick, Maine, commanded the 20th Maine. Chamberlain was to become the unlikely "savior" of the Union army.

As the bluecoats advanced up the slopes of the hill to take position they began taking Confederate artillery fire. Dodging the exploding shells and shattered tree branches, 386 men and their officers from Maine clambered up the slopes and went into line amid the boulders that jutted out from the hill. "All but the drummer boys and hospital

Captain Matthew Talbot Nunnally, Co H, 11th Georgia Infantry was killed in the fighting for the Devil's Den.

Confederate infantry captain's frock coat has Virginia state buttons.

1ˢᵗ New York Light Independent Battery in the Wheatfield.

attendants" were poised to defend the position. Chamberlain arranged his men into line and refused the flank by adjusting several companies to form a right angle with the main line. Chamberlain completed his dispositions just as Confederate Colonel William C. Oates led his own 15ᵗʰ Alabama, accompanied by the 47ᵗʰ Alabama, up the slopes to attack.

Chamberlain's men opened fire as the Confederates approached within fifty yards of their position. The devastating volley, "the most destructive fire I ever saw," according to Oates, staggered the Alabamians, who fell back to regroup. In the next two hours, Oates and his men made five desperate attacks, each time falling just short of breaking Chamberlain's line, which they briefly pierced, before being driven back. Fatigue from long marching and hard fighting, coupled with lack of water began to take its toll. On the Federal side, Chamberlain's men were running out of ammunition and hastened to gather rounds from the cartridge boxes of the dead and wounded lying around.

Major Homer Stoughton's 2ⁿᵈ United States Sharpshooters, who had been skirmishing with the advancing Confederates, were steadily falling back from their post on the left of the III Corps. The

"HE DIED IN A GOOD CAUSE AND LIKE A SOLDIER."

One of the touching stories to emerge from the fight in the Wheatfield was the story of Lieutenant William Fisher, Co. G, 10th United States Infantry. Fisher was among the youngest officers in the army. At just seventeen years of age he was mustered into the U.S. Regulars as a second lieutenant in 1861. At Gettysburg, when the V Corps charged into the Wheatfield, the youth was shot in the chest. Two of his comrades were wounded as they tried to carry him to safety, but Lieutenant Fisher died almost immediately. After the battle he was hastily buried in a shallow grave. His comrades, Private John Buchan, and 1st Sergeant Terance McCabe marked his grave and contacted William's father, Isaac Fisher. Buchan wrote to Isaac about his son, "he was as cool in the battle as he was out of it and as brave a man as there is in the regiment. There was not one man in the regiment but what thought a great deal of him…"

Captain E.B. Bush wrote, "he died in a good cause and like a soldier." Isaac Fisher brought William's body home. Among the items taken with him were the makeshift headstone, crafted from a cigar box, an identification toe tag and a hand drawn map showing the location of Fisher's grave.

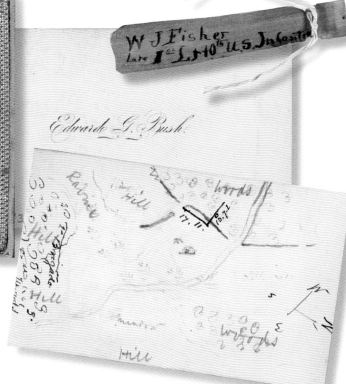

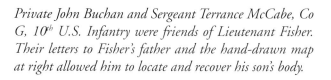

Private John Buchan and Sergeant Terrance McCabe, Co G, 10th U.S. Infantry were friends of Lieutenant Fisher. Their letters to Fisher's father and the hand-drawn map at right allowed him to locate and recover his son's body.

sharpshooters were successively driven from positions on Big Round Top, into the valley and then up the slopes of Little Round Top. They gave ground grudgingly while delaying the advance of Hood's leading units. Under the constant pressure of the Confederate advance, the sharpshooters made their way up the slope of Little Round Top and connected with Co B of the 20th Maine, lending support to the flank defenses on the extreme Union left.

As the Confederates prepared to make another assault, Chamberlain made a desperate decision. Knowing that his ammunition was short and that the stamina of his men was waning under the strain of battle and the physical exertion of hand to hand combat, he opted to counter-attack. The colonel rose up and positioning himself near the colors, uttered the command, "Fix Bayonets!" According to Chamberlain, that word was enough. "It ran like fire along the line…and rose into a shout." Chamberlain's men then charged down the slope while wheeling to the right. The impact of the charge took all of the momentum out of the Confederate attack. Chamberlain's 200 survivors drove Oates' Alabamians down the slopes of Little Round Top, capturing scores of them. The ferocity of the attack was decisive. The 20th Maine drove the Confederates from the slopes of Little Round Top, dispersing the remainder, Oates included, who fled to shelter in a disorganized body.

The crisis for possession of Little Round Top had passed. The Union flank was secured except for skirmish fire and sniping from Devil's Den which continued into the darkness. "Night began settling around us," wrote Valerius C. Giles of the 4th Texas, "but the carnage went on. There seemed to be a viciousness in the very air we breathed." The battle in this part of the field died down. The Confederates would have to try again elsewhere.

As the fighting continued along the line, the battle extended into George Rose's wheatfield. The combat here was concurrent with the fighting in the Peach Orchard and the Devil's Den and Little Round Top sectors. The Wheatfield saw furious see-saw fighting which lasted several hours and would consume the remaining daylight. III Corps regiments of Colonel Regis de Trobriand's Brigade were fighting near the stone wall. Here the 17th Maine withstood the relentless attacks of Brigadier General George T. Anderson's Brigade. "This stone wall was a great protection and the Rebels were straining every nerve to get possession of it for the same purpose. So we held it until our ammunition was exhausted..." wrote John Haley of the 17th Maine.

The III Corps units began giving ground. Units from Hancock's II Corps were supporting them on the right. The initial Confederate onslaught staggered the Union defenders, but the field changed hands several times during the course of the afternoon. Many of the finest units in both armies engaged and thousands of men fell. The 5th New Hampshire, for example, went into action with 177 men and lost eighty-six killed and wounded. Among the slain was Colonel Edward Cross, originally colonel of the regiment, now commanding a brigade. The famed Irish Brigade and Brigadier General Samuel Zook's Brigade drove off Kershaw's Brigade at the stony hill, but were subsequently driven away themselves. The Rose Barn was converted into a makeshift field hospital during the battle.

By late afternoon, the third division of the V Corps, led by Brigadier General Samuel Crawford, charged into the bloody field. Crawford's Pennsylvania Reserves broke the momentum of Confederate successes and drove them back. Caldwell's Brigade was forced back, but Romeyn Ayres' U.S. Regulars went into the fray and stalled the Confederate advance. The Regulars paid heavily for their action, taking more than 800 casualties. Continued fighting caused Ayres to order his Regulars back, abandoning the Wheatfield to the Confederates. Fighting here ended for the day as both sides reorganized their lines.

Meantime Lafayette McLaws' Division, consisting of the brigades of Barksdale, Kershaw, Semmes and Wofford advanced against the exposed III Corps near its salient around the Peach Orchard. Brigadier General Joseph Kershaw led his South Carolina Brigade into combat against the Peach Orchard

position. Kershaw wrote, "In my center-front was a stone farm-house (Rose's) with a barn also of stone. These buildings were about five hundred yards from our position and on a line with the crest of the Peach Orchard hill. The Federal infantry was posted along the front of the orchard, and also on the face looking toward Rose's. Six of their batteries were in position, three at the orchard near the crest of the hill, and the others about two hundred yards in rear... Behind Rose's was a morass and on the right of that, a stone wall running parallel with our line, some two hundred yards from Rose's. Beyond the morass was a stony hill covered with heavy timber and thick undergrowth, interspersed with boulders and large fragments of rock extending some distance toward the Federal line... (by) which a

George Bowen, 12th U.S. Infantry and fragment of the regimental flag.

narrow road led in the direction of (Little Round Top). Looking down this road from Rose's a large wheat-field was seen. In rear of the wheat-field... a heavy force of Federals (were) posted in line behind a stone wall."

Kershaw's attack was met with stiff resistance. Federal batteries stationed in the Peach Orchard wreaked havoc on his flanks as he advanced. When Barksdale's advance on Kershaw's right threatened the safety of Battery E, 1st Rhode Island Light Artillery, the 114th Pennsylvania, Collis' Zouaves, advanced into

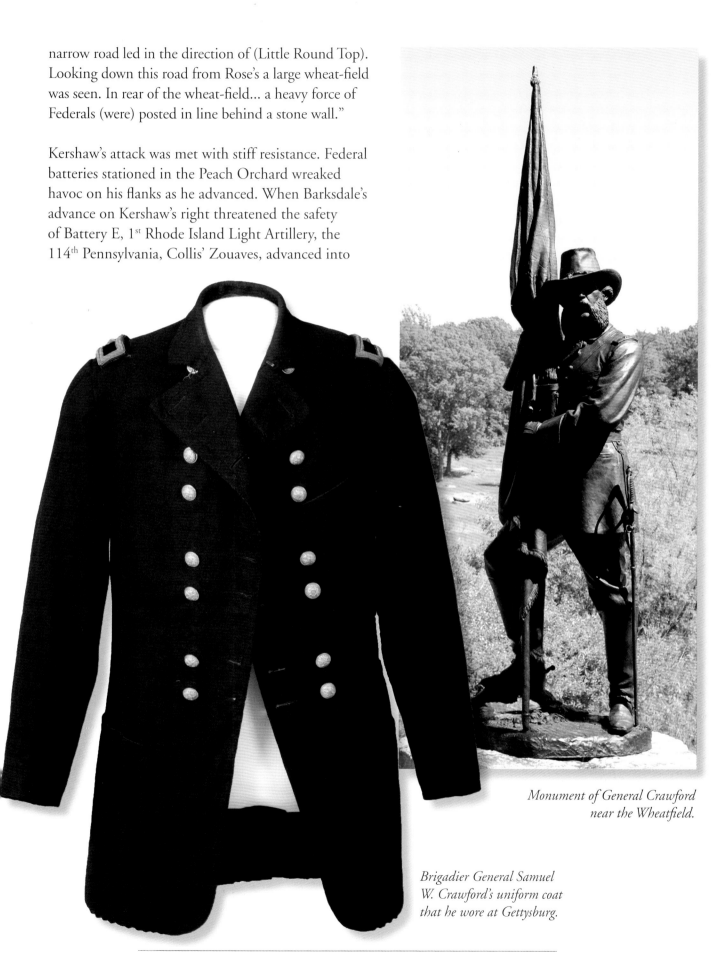

Monument of General Crawford near the Wheatfield.

Brigadier General Samuel W. Crawford's uniform coat that he wore at Gettysburg.

Federal artillery horse team driver.

The first position of the 9th Massachusetts Battery is marked by these two cannon and monument along the Wheatfield Road. It was across the field beyond the fence that the 9ᵗʰ fought its rearguard action until it came to the red brick Trostle barn seen just above the left cannon barrel. Here, in a last ditch effort, much of the battery was overrun.

Lieutenant Christopher Erickson, 9ᵗʰ Massachusetts Battery was mortally wounded at the Trostle farm.

"THE GROUND, EVERY FOOT OF IT, WAS COVERED, WITH MEN AND HORSES..."

The 9ᵗʰ Massachusetts Battery was one of the Union batteries stationed along the Wheatfield Road in a desperate effort to forestall the Confederate attack. But the Confederate advance was relentless. It fell to the 9ᵗʰ Massachusetts Battery, which pulled back to the Trostle Farm, to act as rear guard as the remaining Federal batteries pulled out of line. The 9ᵗʰ Massachusetts Battery was given the grim order to hold its ground at all hazards to cover the withdrawal, an order which spelled its doom. As the battery came under fire from Confederate artillery posted in the fields, Confederate riflemen felled the battery horses, immobilizing the battery's guns. Barksdale's brigade swarmed over the defenders. "Bullets were coming into our midst from many directions," recalled Captain John Bigelow. In the desperate fighting that ensued many of the men of the battery were killed and wounded. "I then saw the Confederates swarming in our right flank, some standing on the limber chests and firing at the gunners," wrote Bigelow. "The ground, every foot of it was covered with men, horses, clothing, cartridge boxes, canteens, guns, bayonets, scattered cartridges, cannon balls everywhere…" David Brett wrote his wife that "it is a meracle that we were not all killed we lost 45 horses the sharp shooters done the work…" The Union positions near the Peach Orchard dissolved and the fighting moved on towards the Wheatfield. Dead from both sides covered the ground. The Confederate onslaught continued on, across the Emmitsburg Road.

the Sherfy farmyard to protect the battery. A fierce firefight ensued between the Mississippians and the Zouaves. Groups of men were knocked out of the ranks. The historian of Kershaw's Brigade wrote, "Men fell here and there from the deadly minnie-balls, while great gaps or swaths were swept away in our ranks by shells from the batteries…" As additional units got involved, fighting swirled around the Sherfy House. Finally, the ferocity of the Confederate attack overwhelmed the dwindling defenders who ran for

Battery C, 5th U.S. commanded by Lieutenant Gulian Weir defended Cemetery Ridge and lost three guns while trying to withdraw. Weir was wounded, but never recovered from the shame of losing his guns. He committed suicide in 1886.

Private Edward Burke, Battery C, 5th U.S. Artillery.

"The Last Full Measure" depicts the forlorn charge of Colonel William Colvill's 1st Minnesota Volunteer Infantry. Hancock ordered this undermanned regiment to attack a brigade. The valiant but doomed charge stalled the Confeder attack, buying Hancock the time he needed to send in reserve The 1st Minnesota lost 215 men out of 262 engaged.

Tintype of Sergeant Patrick Henry Taylor and Isaac Taylor, Co E, 1ˢᵗ Minnesota Volunteer Infantry. Isaac was killed in action on July 2.

safety, in the words of Sergeant Edward Bowen of the 114th Pennsylvania, leaving the Emmitsburg Road "covered with our dead and wounded." Few of the regiment could muster in after the attack.

In the emergency created by the collapse of Sickles' position, and the furious fighting in the Wheatfield and at Little Round Top, General Hancock desperately needed to re-establish a defensive line on Cemetery Ridge, which was being advanced upon by Anderson's Division. "From Round Top to near the Cemetery stretches an uninterrupted field of conflict," wrote Frank Haskell. Hancock attempted to have elements of the shattered III Corps, under General Alexander Humphreys, form line on Cemetery Ridge. Until these men could take position and reinforcements could be brought to the threatened position, however, someone needed to occupy the advancing Confederates. Hancock ordered the first regiment he could find to charge into the attacking Southerners. What Hancock needed was time. As fate would have it, that crucial time was to be bought with the life's blood of

In the deepening gloom of the evening woods, Southern infantry attacks dug-in Union positions. They will wrest from the Federals some of the breastworks...but not all. The fate of who will hold Culp's Hill would be decide the following day.

the undermanned 1st Minnesota Volunteers, whose eight companies numbered just 262 men. Hancock observed the regiment crouching along the west bank of Plum Run in support of a Federal battery. "My God, are these all the troops we have here?" exclaimed Hancock, thunderstruck at the scarcity of men available. Despite the lack of strength, Hancock was resolved. He later remarked, "I would have ordered that regiment in if I had known that every man would be killed. It had to be done." Thus he ordered Colonel William Colvill to advance and take the colors of the foremost Confederate regiment.

Captain James Young Co C and the National colors of the 60th New York. The 60th New York was engaged in the heavy fighting on Culp's Hill and captured two Confederate flags.

The meaning of this order was not lost on those fated to make the advance. William Lochren recalled that "Every man realized in an instant what that order meant—death or wounds to us all…" Colonel Colvill ordered his men to go forward. The Minnesotans attacked three regiments of Cadmus Wilcox's brigade, some 1,100 strong. The Rebels were barely 350 yards away and closing that distance quickly. The unexpected and ferocious assault stymied the Confederates. In a furious firefight lasting just a few minutes, the regiment lost 215 men killed and wounded. This eighty-two

From the edge of the town of Gettysburg came a ferocious attack on the Union defenses on Cemetery Hill. In the quickly falling light of July 2, Confederate brigades overran the infantry at the base of the hill who in turn fled through the batteries at its crest. Artillerymen and infantry fought a savage hand-to-hand combat until Union reinforcements rushed through the town's cemetery and pushed back the gray tide.

percent casualty rate in a single assault was the costliest of the war. The ferocious attack broke through the first line of Rebels and stalled their advance, albeit briefly. In the ensuing combat the Minnesotans captured the flag of the 28th Virginia Infantry. The precious minutes bought by the sacrifice of this regiment allowed Hancock to fashion a reserve line to meet the main Confederate thrust against Cemetery Ridge. Later only forty-seven men of the 1st Minnesota were present for duty. They participated in the defense of Pickett's Charge the following day.

As darkness fell, fighting broke out on Cemetery Hill. General William Barksdale's Brigade advanced past Wilcox's Brigade to assault the hill. Colonel David Lang's Florida Brigade was also making its attack. A brigade of Federals from Alexander Hays' II Corps division stymied the Confederate advance. Colonel George Willard's brigade halted Barksdale. Both Willard and Barksdale were killed in the fighting. Lieutenant Gulian Weir, commanding a battery of the 5th U.S. Artillery was wounded and lost three of his guns in the fighting with Lang's Floridians. "The fire all along the crest is terrific, and it is a wonder how any human thing could have stood before it," recalled Haskell. Additional units of the II Corps arrived in time to drive off the Confederates to end the fighting here. Later in the evening, on East Cemetery Hill another furious Confederate attack was successfully repulsed.

On the right flank of the Union line, the battle was raging at Culp's Hill, a heavily wooded knoll lying south and east of the town of Gettysburg. Standing 627 feet high, the hill slopes westward where it connects to East Cemetery Hill.

On the afternoon of July 1, Federal refugees of the I and XI Corps made their way to Cemetery Ridge. General Winfield Scott Hancock, commander of the II Corps had been empowered by Meade to take command of the field at Gettysburg. Hancock wasted little time in notifying Howard, who begrudgingly yielded command (Howard ranked Hancock by seniority). Hancock ordered a Federal battery to go to Culp's Hill and forestall Confederate efforts to take the hill, thereby anchoring the Union flank. A Confederate presence on the heights would force Hancock to abandon the line being strengthened on Cemetery Hill. In addition to the artillery, the remnants of the Iron Brigade wearily made their way to the slopes of the hill and began entrenching.

The Confederates of Johnson's Division of Ewell's Corps arrived on the field exhausted after their forced march to Gettysburg. Ewell ordered a reconnaissance of the hill, but did not make any concerted effort to seize it. This decision was to have unintended consequences for the Southerners. It was not until nearly midnight when Ewell ordered Johnson to seize the hill. Johnson demurred with the knowledge that Federal forces occupied the hill in force.

During the afternoon of July 2, the Union XII spent its time building breastworks. About 6:00 p.m., Brigadier General George S. Greene's Brigade of five New York regiments found itself alone on the hill when the other XII Corps units were ordered away to bolster Sickles' collapsing line. Greene, the oldest general in the Federal army, had the foresight to order his 1,500 men to entrench, thus fortifying their position on this critical hill. Late in the afternoon, Greene's Brigade was assaulted by the division of Major General Edward "Alleghany" Johnson. In a furious action that lasted well into the darkness, the Confederates were repeatedly driven back.

Among the Confederates who attacked Greene's Brigade on Culp's Hill was the 2nd Maryland. This regiment was assigned to Brigadier General George H. Steuart's Brigade. Following the arduous trek to Gettysburg, the men arrived on the evening of July 1, marching past the carnage of the first days' battle

As the bruised but not broken Army of the Potomac collapsed to the ground on the evening of July 2, their commander, George Meade, made the fateful decision to stay and continue the fight at Gettysburg.

and pausing to rest in the streets of the town before going into line along the Hanover Pike. On the evening of July 2, at Culp's Hill they participated in Steuart's attack. The Confederates on this part of the line endured an all day wait, able to hear the sounds of attacks on other parts of the field, but ignorant of the outcome of the combat on the other end of the line. Finally they were ordered into action late in the day, attacking Union forces on Culp's Hill, where they overran a portion of the Union fortifications. The Marylanders succeeded in capturing part of the line, but lost more than a hundred men in the bloody fighting, including their commander, Colonel Herbert, who was struck three times.

During the night, as the sounds of battle died away, Meade convened eleven of his senior commanders for a council of war at his headquarters along the Taneytown Road in the Leister House. In a crowded room, clouded with cigar smoke and lit only by candlelight, the commanding generals of the Army of the Potomac determined to hold their ground and await the attacks of the following day. All of the corps commanders were present, reporting on the status of their commands, their supplies, their losses and their readiness to fight. Meade's chief engineer, General Warren, exhausted from his stressful but heroic activities on July 2, nestled on the floor and slept throughout the conference. Much was discussed but the consensus that was reached was that the Army of the Potomac would hold its ground and finish the fight. As the council broke up, Meade turned to General John Gibbon and remarked "If Lee attacks tomorrow, it will be on your front."

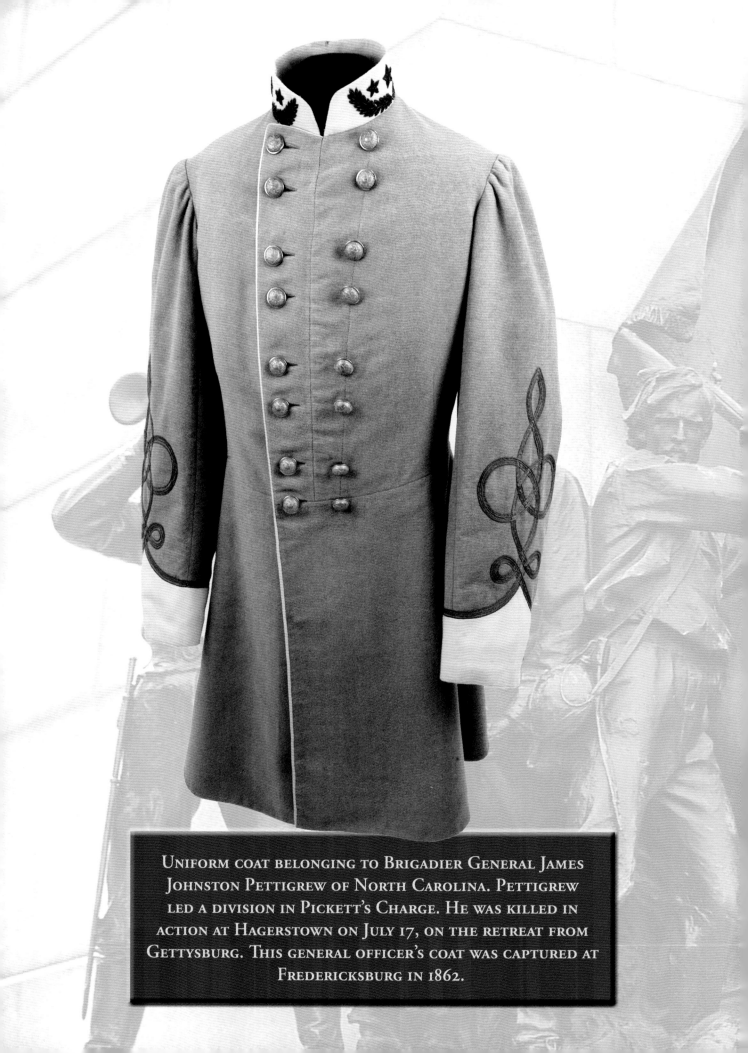

UNIFORM COAT BELONGING TO BRIGADIER GENERAL JAMES
JOHNSTON PETTIGREW OF NORTH CAROLINA. PETTIGREW
LED A DIVISION IN PICKETT'S CHARGE. HE WAS KILLED IN
ACTION AT HAGERSTOWN ON JULY 17, ON THE RETREAT FROM
GETTYSBURG. THIS GENERAL OFFICER'S COAT WAS CAPTURED AT
FREDERICKSBURG IN 1862.

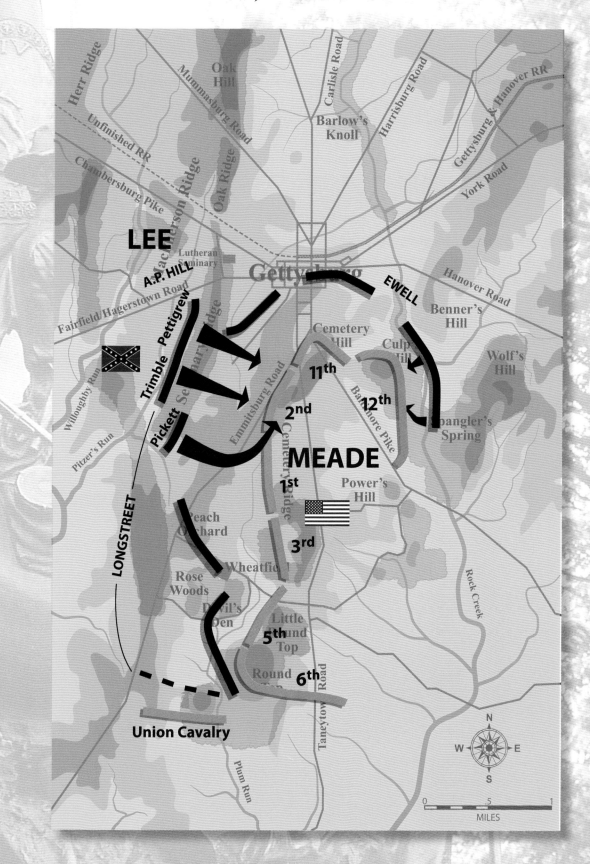

Herr Ridge

Oak Hill

Carlisle Road

Harrisburg Road

Gettysburg & Hanover RR

Unfinished RR

Mummasburg Road

Barlow's Knoll

York Road

Chambersburg Pike

McPherson Ridge

Oak Ridge

LEE

Lutheran Seminary

A.P. HILL

Hanover Road

Gettysburg

EWELL

Fairfield/Hagerstown Road

Benner's Hill

Trimble **Pettigrew**

Cemetery Hill

Culp's Hill

Wolf's Hill

Willoughby Run

Seminary Ridge

11th

Pickett

Emmitsburg Road

2nd

12th

Spangler's Spring

Baltimore Pike

Pitzer's Run

MEADE

1st

Power's Hill

LONGSTREET

Peach Orchard

Cemetery Ridge

3rd

Rock Creek

Rose Woods

Wheatfield

Devil's Den

Little Round Top

5th

6th

Round Top

Taneytown Road

Plum Run

Union Cavalry

N
W   E
S

0   5   1
MILES

orning of July 3 found both armies still on the field and awaiting combat. General Lee was determined to stay and fight the battle to its ultimate conclusion. The Federals had made their plan. Lee initially planned for a resumption of the attacks against the Federal flanks but the failure of General Johnson's Division to exploit the gains of the previous evening forced Lee to reconsider. The furious fighting on Culp's Hill opened the action but the repulse of the Confederates stabilized the activity in that sector of the field. By mid-morning, Lee ordered General Longstreet to do exactly what Meade had predicted—assault the Union center. Lee was determined to make a grand assault meant to finally achieve what had been promised on July 1 and so fleetingly missed on July 2—a Confederate victory. A stressful morning passed by as preparations were made for the grand assault against the Union center.

Easily the most famous action at Gettysburg is the attack known as Pickett's Charge. The duty of making the grand attack against the Federal center fell upon James Longstreet and his corps. Longstreet later wrote that he protested the wisdom of this assault to Lee. "General, I have been a soldier all my life. I have been with soldiers engaged in fights by couples, by squads, companies, regiments, divisions, and armies, and should know, as well as any one, what soldiers can do. It is my opinion that no fifteen thousand men ever arranged for battle can take that position."

The artillery bombardment meant to soften up the Union positions on Cemetery Ridge began at approximately one o'clock in the afternoon and lasted for over one and a half hours, with hundreds of cannons from both armies firing relentlessly upon each other. The Confederate artillery was ineffectual, failing to drive off the Union guns on Cemetery Ridge, but managing to disrupt activities at Meade's headquarters behind it. Union counter-battery fire inflicted casualties upon the Confederates massing for the attack that was to follow the barrage, but failed to silence the long arm of Lee. Finally, as the cannonade dwindled, Colonel Edward Porter Alexander, Longstreet's chief of artillery, reported that the Federal guns seemed to be withdrawing. "If you are going to advance at all, you must come at once…" he advised. (In fact, they had ceased firing to conserve ammunition for the impending attack). The time for the infantry assault had arrived.

Major General Winfield Scott Hancock commanded the Union II Corps. Hancock formed the Union defensive line on Cemetery Ridge on July 1 and defended it against Pickett's Charge on July 3.

Longstreet agonized over giving the order for the assault which he believed in his heart could not succeed. Despite Porter's optimistic assessment, Longstreet was still against making the charge. He could not bring himself to give the command, but only nodded his assent when asked by Pickett, whose division had arrived that morning, if the assault was to proceed. Pickett had been chosen because his division was the largest available force that had not already been engaged. With this silent affirmation, Pickett initiated the most renowned assault of the Civil War.

In addition to Pickett, the divisions of Brigadier General James Johnston Pettigrew (of A.P. Hill's Corps) and Major General Isaac Trimble would spearhead the attack. Pettigrew was replacing the wounded Heth and Trimble was replacing William Dorsey Pender, the two original commanders having received wounds previously in the battle. Nine brigades of Confederate soldiers advanced on the Union lines, covering a front of about a mile. The charge was made over 1400 yards of mostly open ground, making the attackers vulnerable every step of the way to

Each Union army corps had its own distinctive flag. This is the Headquarters flag of Hancock's II Corps.

Longstreet, opposed to Lee's strategy of a frontal assault across nearly a mile of open farm fields, reluctantly gives the order to Pickett to advance in this painting titled, The Burden of Command.

Private Caleb May, 13th North Carolina Infantry was wounded in the attack on Cemetery Ridge. The 13th North Carolina, of Brigadier General A.M. Scales' Brigade, lost seventy-seven percent of its strength in Pickett's Charge.

Compact columns of Southern infantry march stoically forward as Union artillery begins to find the range.

Confederate Pattern 1839 cartridge box, carried by Private John Wells, Co H, 18th North Carolina, killed during Pickett's Charge.

Union artillery, and as they neared the objective, deadly musketry and canister fire. The focus of the attack was a copse of trees on Cemetery Ridge.

Union Colonel Frank Haskell was an eyewitness to the charge and described it as follows: "Every eye could see the enemy's legions, an overwhelming resistless tide of an ocean of armed men sweeping upon us! Regiment after regiment and brigade after brigade move from the woods and rapidly take their places in the line forming the assault. Pickett's proud division with some additional troops hold their right. The first line at short intervals is followed by a second, and that a third succeeds; and columns between support the lines…" It was a grand spectacle that one could not help but to

admire. Major General Winfield Scott Hancock, commanding the Union II Corps which was holding the line atop Cemetery Ridge recalled, "Their lines were formed with a precision and steadiness that exhorted the admiration of the witnesses of that memorable scene."

Bullet-ridden fence rail from the Emmitsburg Pike.

Despite their admiration of the spectacle, the Union defenders did their utmost to destroy it. War is glorious and terrible, its purpose to kill and destroy. The Federals on Cemetery Ridge were all too aware of their duty and they executed it with great effect. Shot and shell from artillery, combined with sustained volleys of musketry made the Confederates pay dearly for every forward step. Captain Henry T. Owen, of the 18th Virginia of Garnett's Brigade recalled that "The destruction of life in the ranks of that advancing host was fearful beyond precedent, officers going down by dozens and the men by scores and fifties." Despite the horrific losses the Confederates advanced relentlessly, taking advantage of momentary cover from swells in the ground to dress their lines, consolidating their front to one-half mile. Steadily, unbelievably, they advanced into the maelstrom of death as they neared the Union lines, making a final, desperate push for the Ridge and the guns upon it.

The last hundred yards before coming to grips with their foe proved to be the deadliest for those in Pickett's Charge. General Garnett, mounted on a bay horse, encourages the remnants of his brigade as an officer who has picked up the fallen flag, rallies the men of his 18th Virginia.

Captain Henry T. Owen, Co C, 18th Virginia Infantry, commanded the regiment after all of the other officers were killed and wounded in Pickett's Charge.

Private John Cassidy, 69th Pennsylvania Volunteers, killed at the Angle on July 3.

Lew Armistead, with hat on sword, crosses the stone wall at 'The Angle'. Woefully few will cross with him, none of whom will escape death or capture.

Confederate Brigadier General Richard B. Garnett had defied orders to dismount, and instead led his brigade on horseback, making him an obvious and conspicuous target. Pickett had cautioned him to move as quickly as possible because he was "going to catch Hell." The general was recovering from an injury and need not have made the assault. Garnett and his brigade neared to within 200 yards of the stone wall when the magnitude of the fire hitting them increased in intensity. Garnett tried to steady what was left of his brigade for the final push into the very faces of the Union defenders. Running, oblivious now to commands to dress the lines, the attackers pushed on. A devastating volley dropped many of them. Garnett's riderless horse, bleeding at the shoulder, was observed fleeing the field. The gallant general's body was never identified.

John Cassidy's bullet torn bible

Private Benjamin Taylor, Co F, 26th North Carolina. The 26th lost 588 out of 800 men fighting the Iron Brigade on July 1. On July 3, it lost an additional 120 men and its flag in Pickett's Charge.

Second Lieutenant Frederick Boland, Co B, 72nd Pennsylvania Volunteers, the Fire Zouave Regiment, defended the Angle.

Once at the wall, General Lewis B. Armistead led his surviving men over it. For a brief instant, victory seemed possible. But Armistead was shot down as he leapt over the wall and placed his hand on a captured artillery piece. His hat, which he had placed upon the tip of his sword, slid down the blade to his hand. He fell amongst his men at the angle in the Union defensive line. All too suddenly the reality and determination of Federal strength slammed down upon the Confederates who had breached the line. There were too few of the gray-clad soldiers to exploit the breach. The furious Federal counterattack compelled many to surrender, rather than retrace their steps across the killing fields. Before the war, Armistead had been good friends in the Old Army with Hancock, whose line he had just breached. He requested a meeting with the II Corps commander only to learn that Hancock, too, had been seriously wounded.

Those who breached the wall were killed or captured. The rest fled. Confederate soldier David Holt, of the 16th Mississippi Infantry recalled that "We fell back over our dead and wounded, with here and there the body of a dead Yankee who had been left from the fighting of the day before. Our batteries did not fire to protect us and the Yanks had it all their own way."

The 10th New York Battalion (The National Zouaves), numbering a scant 98 officers and men, was posted along the Taneytown Road, directly in the rear of their division and near Meade's headquarters, on the reverse slope of Cemetery Ridge. They had skirmished most of the previous day before being ordered to the left of the line to turn back the stragglers from the fighting at Little Round Top and the III Corps. Now, their necessary, if unglamorous duty, was again to force stragglers to return to the battle line and also to take custody of prisoners coming from the front. The battalion was formed in an extended skirmish line, acting as file closers. The men stood ten paces apart in a single line. Here, the men took shelter during the massive artillery duel between Union and Confederate forces that preceded the grand assault that was Pickett's Charge. Laying prone on the reverse slope of the hill, the battalion endured the horrendous bombardment, taking what scant shelter was provided by trees, stone walls and depressions in the ground. Several casualties were sustained during this bombardment. According to adjutant Lieutenant Charles W. Cowtan, the regiment was kept constantly busy stopping the stragglers ebbing away from the main line on Cemetery Hill.

During the crisis at the angle, at the zenith of Pickett's Charge, the battalion was personally ordered to the front by Union commander General George G. Meade, as every man was needed to stem the breach made by Pickett's determined Confederates. As the 10th New York Battalion neared the front, in the midst of the battle smoke, it was met by a surge of Confederate soldiers. The battalion braced for hand to hand fighting, but the crisis had passed. These were beaten men who had already surrendered and were making their way to the rear, or throwing themselves to the ground for safety. The 10th New York Battalion took custody of these prisoners, numbering 360 officers and 1,510 enlisted men and escorted them on the long march to the Union rear.

Confederate 1st National flag captured from a Confederate officer during Pickett's Charge by Major Walter A. Van Rensselaer, 20th New York State Militia.

.58 caliber Richmond Armory rifle-musket carried by Private William D. Holt, Co K, 18th Virginia Infantry, captured at Gettysburg. Note WD Holt carved in left side of stock.

Pickett's attack failed with a loss of greater than fifty per cent. Garnett's brigade lost 941 men and officers out of 1,427 who made the charge. The loss had been appalling. "Outside the wall," recalled Union artillery commander Colonel Charles Wainwright, "the enemy really lay in heaps…There was about

Captain John D. H. Robinson, Co E, 13ᵗʰ Alabama Infantry.

Uniform jacket and vest of the 10ᵗʰ New York Volunteer Infantry.

The 10ᵗʰ New York, the National Zouaves acted as provost guards during the Gettysburg Campaign. At Pickett's Charge they captured 360 officers and 1,150 enlisted men who survived the assault.

A pattern 1853 British Enfield rifle-musket, carried by Private John A. Fallin, Co E, 23rd Virginia Infantry, found on slopes of Culp's Hill. The closeup shows his name and unit carved in the stock.

an acre of ground here where you could not walk without stepping over the bodies." As Lee viewed the shattered remnants of the attacking force as they made their way back to the Confederate lines, he rode out to meet them. "It is all my fault," he assured them. When he was ordered to prepare his division for a likely counterattack, the teary-eyed Pickett cried, "General, I have no division."

The Federals on Cemetery Ridge were as disorganized by the attack as had been the Confederates. Though Longstreet prepared what was left of his forces to meet an anticipated counterattack, none came. Meade demurred from making the expected attack despite having the unbloodied VI Corps in reserve. Enough was enough for now, seemed to be his thought process. For the Confederates, their high water mark had come and ebbed away. They would never again have such an opportunity on Northern soil. The attack known as Pickett's Charge remains a source of study and controversy and is arguably the subject of more what ifs than any other action of the Civil War.

Novelist William Faulkner immortalized this line of thinking in *Intruder in the Dust*. "For every Southern boy fourteen years old, not once but whenever he wants it, there is the instant when it's still not yet two o'clock on that July afternoon in 1863, the brigades are in position behind the rail fence, the guns are laid and ready in the woods and the furled flags are already loosened to break out and Pickett himself with his long oiled ringlets and his hat in one hand probably and his sword in the other looking up the hill waiting for Longstreet to give the word and it's all in the balance, it hasn't happened yet, it hasn't even begun yet, it not only hasn't begun yet but there is still time for it not to begin against that position and those circumstances which made more men than Garnett and Kemper and Armistead and Wilcox look grave yet it's going to begin, we all know that, we have come too far with too much at stake and that moment doesn't need even a fourteen-year-old boy to think This time. Maybe this time with all this much to lose than all this much to gain: Pennsylvania, Maryland, the world, the golden dome of Washington itself to crown with desperate and unbelievable victory the desperate gamble, the cast made two years ago."

Infantryman of the 2nd Maryland and the regiment's monument on Culp's Hill.

CULP'S HILL

On July 3, the 2nd Maryland again attacked. Steuart's Brigade formed at right angles to the entrenchments they had taken the previous night and charged the Federal position, making a direct frontal assault. The advance led them into an open field, two hundred yards from the Union line. The Federal position was heavily manned and the fire they brought to bear on the Marylanders was devastating. The 2nd Maryland was decimated, losing 189 men, almost half of those engaged. In two days' fighting they sustained more than 300 casualties.

In addition to the attacks at Culp's Hill and Cemetery Ridge, Lee ordered Jeb Stuart's cavalry to get into the Union rear to exploit whatever advantage was gained as a result of Pickett's Charge. In East Cavalry Field, Stuart's Confederate cavalry attacked and was repulsed by Federal cavalry commanded by General David McM. Gregg. Here, in a glorious charge, Brigadier General George A. Custer won everlasting fame. The boy general had been promoted just days before the battle, making the jump from captain to brigadier general. The Confederate repulse here squelched any chance for Lee to gain a foothold in rear of the Union line.

This Confederate officer's frock coat was worn by 2nd Lieutenant Samuel G. Bonn of Co F, 1st Maryland cavalry Battalion, C.S.A. The 1st Maryland was assigned courier duty and as artillery support at Gettysburg.

Confederate cavalry bugler

In South Cavalry Field, an unnecessary and disastrous charge, ordered by Judson Kilpatrick, led to the death of newly promoted Brigadier General Elon Farnsworth, of Illinois. Farnsworth protested Kilpatrick's foolhardy order to attack. When Kilpatrick mockingly questioned Farnsworth's bravery, the infuriated young general made the fatal and futile attack. The young commander proved his point and saved his honor, but lost his life in doing it. The charge was pointless and brought no beneficial result to either side.

Union cavalry thunder forward at the charge.

THE AFTERMATH

The day after the battle, many of the survivors explored the battlefield. Franklin Sawyer of the 8th Ohio described what he saw: "Everywhere were the evidences of a fierce struggle. Dismounted guns, exploded caissons and limbers, hundreds of dead horses, piles of broken and bent muskets, splintered trees, broken tomb stones at Cemetery Hill, demolished walls, riddled houses and barns met the eye. The ground was plowed and cross-plowed by cannon balls, which had swept through our lines in every direction."

Union hospital steward's uniform jacket with distinctive green chevron and medical corps insignia.

Prior to the battle, Gettysburg was a town of some 2,400 inhabitants. After three days of horrific conflict, 51,000 soldiers were counted among the dead, wounded, missing and those taken prisoner. Thousands of dead and dying horses and mules littered the landscape. "Dead soldiers were everywhere," recalled one resident of the town. On every part of the battlefield, burial details and civilians recorded grisly descriptions of the number and attitude of the dead. "For seven days it literally ran blood, "one nurse remembered. For several months after the battle, Gettysburg was overwhelmed with the burden of caring for the wounded, burying the dead and disposing of the rotting animal carcasses. Numerous farms, houses, hotels, taverns and churches were used as hospitals. Wagonloads of amputated arms and legs left these makeshift hospitals for burial in trenches.

The shattered landscape bore mute testimony to the savagery human beings wrought upon each other. Many houses bore the scars of bullets and artillery shot and shell. Fences and barns were destroyed, fields were trampled and orchards were devastated. Broken and abandoned muskets, accouterments of every description and shell fragments littered the ground. Unexploded shells still proved lethal to souvenir hunters. The residents of the town had their work cut out for them trying to return to some semblance of normalcy. But Gettysburg would never be the same.

The Union Army medical corps, commanded by Dr. Jonathan Letterman, established a field hospital system to oversee the care of the wounded. More than a hundred medical officers from the army, a third of whom were surgeons, remained to care for the wounded. Camp Letterman was the field headquarters hospital that oversaw the treatment of the more than 22,000 wounded men left behind by both armies as they left the area to continue the campaign. Letterman, a native Pennsylvanian, was a professional army surgeon with many years of practical experience. In a time when medical science was still relatively primitive, Letterman was an innovator who developed an organized ambulance system and an efficient method for gathering and caring for the sick and wounded of the army. His herculean efforts saved many from death after the battle.

Still, despite the best efforts of the Union and Confederate surgeons, approximately 10,000 men died as a result of the battle. Many were buried on the farms or in the yards of houses and other buildings that served as makeshift hospitals in the emergency. Human remains were buried wherever they were found, but the carcasses of the dead animals were piled up

A crude wooden crutch and a pocket lancet, a double-edged scalpel used by army surgeons.

and burned. The stench from the battlefield was almost unbearable and could be smelled from afar. Residents coped by using camphor or smelling salts, and interring the dead as quickly as possible.

The thousands of burials dotting the landscape turned the town and its environs into one vast cemetery. Many of the graves were shallow, hasty trenches that were uncovered with the first heavy rain. The result was a countryside abounding with untold horrors at every turn. Pennsylvania Governor Andrew Curtin reacted to this gruesome state of affairs by promising that the state would provide funding for a decent burial of the Union slain. The citizens of Adams County were hard pressed to properly inter so many fallen in such a short period of time. A prominent local attorney, David Wills, devised a plan and with the financial and political support of the state, a professional landscaper was hired to design and lay out the cemetery. These efforts alleviated the situation and proper burials began. Ultimately more than 3500 of the Union slain were re-interred in the new seventeen acre cemetery, the Soldiers' National Cemetery. The Soldiers' National Cemetery was formally dedicated on November 19, 1863. Amid a town still bearing the scars of the battle and where wounded were still being treated, thousands of spectators gathered to hear the renowned speaker, Edward Everett, deliver the dedication. Seemingly an afterthought, the organizers also invited President Abraham Lincoln to participate in the ceremonies. As Commander in Chief, it was felt that his presence was required.

Confederate Major Simon Baruch was the surgeon of the 13th Mississippi Infantry of Longstreet's Corps.

This black leather medical bag was found abandoned on the field after the battle. The paper label inside the lid lists its now missing contents, perhaps used up and discarded while caring for the wounded.

THIS IS A CONFEDERATE ARMY SURGEON'S FROCK COAT. THE DARK COLLAR AND CUFFS DENOTE THE MEDICAL SERVICES AND THE SINGLE STAR ON THE COLLAR DENOTES THE RANK OF MAJOR, THE USUAL RANK FOR AN ARMY SURGEON.

DEDICATION

Gettysburg will always be remembered for the great battle fought there but even more for the "few appropriate remarks" made there by President Abraham Lincoln on November 19, 1863. President Lincoln had been seeking an opportunity to address the nation for some time, to clarify the war aims to a wearying North and to redefine its purpose and meaning. When he received the belated invitation to speak, Lincoln was given the ideal opportunity to make known his thoughts. He had little more than two weeks to compose his speech, but the ideals expressed therein had been crafted over a lifetime. President Lincoln felt the occasion was important and meaningful enough to leave Washington to go to the scene of the battle. The crowd in attendance was estimated at over 15,000 including six state governors. Lincoln's speech, which he delivered in just two and a half minutes, received mixed reactions from partisan newspapers, along party lines. But the words resonated in the press and the speech was destined to become immortal, renowned as his most famous speech.

The Gettysburg Address

"Four score and seven years ago our fathers brought forth on this continent, a new nation, conceived in Liberty, and dedicated to the proposition that all men are created equal. Now we are engaged in a great civil war, testing whether that nation, or any nation so conceived and so dedicated, can long endure. We are met on a great battle-field of that war. We have come to dedicate a portion of that field, as a final resting place for those who here gave their lives that that nation might live. It is altogether fitting and proper that we should do this. But, in a larger sense, we can not dedicate — we can not consecrate — we can not hallow — this ground. The brave men, living and dead, who struggled here, have consecrated it, far above our poor power to add or detract. The world will little note, nor long remember what we say here, but it can never forget what they did here. It is for us the living, rather, to be dedicated here to the unfinished work which they who fought here have thus far so nobly advanced. It is rather for us to be here dedicated to the great task remaining before us — that from these honored dead we take increased devotion to that cause for which they gave the last full measure of devotion — that we here highly resolve that these dead shall not have died in vain — that this nation, under God, shall have a new birth of freedom — and that government of the people, by the people, for the people, shall not perish from the earth."

❧ COMMEMORATION ❧

A June 1897 photo of Major William M. Robbins standing by the stake depicting the spot where Colonel Isaac E. Avery fell on the evening of July 2, in the attack on Cemetery Hill.

Today, Gettysburg National Military Park is the nation's single most visited national battlefield, drawing two million visitors annually. It did not take long for the battlefield to gain its status. As one of the first five national military parks created, Gettysburg was recognized early on as being a pivotal place and event in our history. The soldiers who fought there, both North and South, sought out the battlefields of their youth to bring understanding and meaning to the sacrifice they had made and also to help in the reconciliation of the two sections of the now re-united nation. Monument commissions from every state walked the hallowed fields at Gettysburg to mark where they fought, where their comrades fell and where great acts were performed. The result was a landscape dotted and marked with magnificent monuments, and edifices, silent sentinels to what could now be remembered as glory once the immediacy of the pain and loss had passed.

The importance of the battlefield was such that as early as 1864 The Gettysburg Battlefield Memorial Association was formed to purchase and preserve the land, and place markers to commemorate the heroic deeds and events of the battle. By 1883 one author wrote about the battle that "the interest… is steadily increasing, as is attested by the constantly swelling number of visitors and by the erection of memorial structures in commemoration of the great deeds of the heroes who here gave their lives…" The advent of the Grand Army of the Republic and its annual reunions added impetus to the desire to do something to preserve the fields. Residents also contributed to the commemoration of the battlefield, donating or selling their property to the Memorial Association. By 1895, some 500 acres were acquired. Finally, an act of Congress, fostered by legislation penned by General Dan Sickles, turned ownership of the land over to the Federal Government, making Gettysburg one of the first five National Military Parks.

The Battle of Gettysburg has been commemorated in many ways. The establishment of the park itself and the hundreds of monuments and plaques that decorate the landscape are readily apparent. These were in large part erected by the veterans themselves, or those who remembered the fallen as a testament to their service. More than 5,000 books have been written about the battle, with new titles being added to the list every year. These are avidly read by scholars, military historians, Civil War buffs and the public at large, hungry for historic knowledge. The books cover everything from detailed campaign analyses, controversies, and unit histories to minutiae such as specific weapons and uniforms worn by the soldiers. *Gettysburg Magazine*, a scholarly journal covering all aspects of the battle has been published for more than twenty years, covering virtually every detail and controversy of the battle. Gettysburg is the subject of movies, documentaries, television shows (like the *Twilight Zone*) re-enactments, war games and miniature soldier enthusiasts. It is also the subject of numerous paintings and sculptures, both historic and modern. Perhaps the most spectacular of the hundreds of paintings depicting the battle is the Gettysburg Cyclorama.

The General John Buford Monument.

The Gettysburg Cyclorama, panel 1

Charles A. Hale of the 5th New Hampshire Volunteer Infantry fought at Gettysburg. After the war he was a licensed battlefield guide and traveled with the Cyclorama as a lecturer and interpreter of the painting.

The Gettysburg Cyclorama is a massive 360 degree rendition of the battle created by Paul Philippoteaux in 1883-84 for the sum of $50,000. The restored version now on display is 377 feet long and 42 feet high, weighing four tons. It depicts the action on July 3, 1863, Pickett's Charge, the climax of the battle. The stunning artwork is enhanced with military props and foliage, adding depth and illusion to the painting with a three dimensional fade in foreground. Several versions of the Gettysburg Cyclorama were produced as well as a number of other Civil War battles and other events. Today, the Cyclorama stands as a monument to the battle as well as to the artistic vision of the 19th Century.

The Gettysburg Cyclorama, panel 2

Today, when urban sprawl threatens hallowed ground at every turn, the importance and relevance of battlefields like Gettysburg has increased. More than ever the appreciation of the battle and what it represents are vital to an understanding of the American identity. The National Park Service has recognized this and has gone to great lengths to reach out to a new generation of Americans. The new museum and visitor's center is geared toward educating the novice to the study of Civil War battles and explaining the significance of Gettysburg as an important part of the whole. More serious students and historians can avail themselves of the collections and view specific artifacts and documents more easily than ever before. Thus, both the novice and the professional can make the maximum use of the resources of the Museum and its holdings. New technologies, combined with artifacts of the battle and a restoration of the historic landscape all combine to give visitors the best interpretation yet of the Battle of Gettysburg.

The Gettysburg Cyclorama, panel 3

❧ BIBLIOGRAPHY ❧

Adelman, Garry E. and Timothy H. Smith, *Devil's Den A History and Guide*, (Thomas Publications, Gettysburg, 1997)

Adelman, Garry E., *Little Round Top A Detailed Tour Guide*, (Thomas Publications, Gettysburg, 2000).

Adkin, Mark, *The Gettysburg Companion: A Complete Guide to America's Most Famous Battle*, (Stackpole Books, Mechanicsburg, 2008)

Archer, John M., *East Cemetery Hill at Gettysburg*, (Thomas Publications, Gettysburg, 1997)

Archer, John M., *Culp's Hill at Gettysburg*, (Thomas Publications, Gettysburg, 2002)

Ayers, Edward L., *In the Presence of Mine Enemies*, (W.W. Norton and Co., New York, 2003)

Bandy, Ken and Florence Freeland, *The Gettysburg Papers*, (Morningside Bookshop, Dayton, 1986)

Boardman, Sue and Kathryn Porch, *The Battle of Gettysburg Cyclorama, A History and Guide,* (Thomas Publications, Gettysburg, 2008)

Byrne, Frank L. and Andrew T. Weaver, editors, *Haskell of Gettysburg: His Life and Civil War Papers*, (Kent State University Press, Kent, 1989)

Campbell, Eric A., *"A Grand Terrible Dramma," From Gettysburg to Petersburg: The Civil War Letters of Charles Wellington Reed*, (Fordham University Press, New York, 2000)

Cockrell, Thomas D. and Michael B. Ballard, editors, *A Mississippi Rebel in the Army of Northern Virginia: The Civil War Memoirs of Private David Holt*, (Louisiana State University Press, Baton Rouge, 1995)

Coco, Gregory A., *A Strange and Blighted Land. Gettysburg: The Aftermath of a Battle*, (Thomas Publications, Gettysburg, 1995)

The Gettysburg Cyclorama, panel 4

Coco, Gregory A., *Wasted Valor, The Confederate Dead at Gettysburg*, (Thomas Publications, Gettysburg, 1990)

Coco, Gregory A., *A Vast Sea of Misery: A Guide to the Union and Confederate Field Hospitals at Gettysburg, July 1-Nov 20, 1863*, (Thomas Publications, Gettysburg, 1988)

Coddington, Edwin B., *The Gettysburg Campaign*, (Charles Scribner's Sons, New York, 1968)

Cowtan, Charles W., *Services of the Tenth New York Volunteers, National Zouaves in the War of the Rebellion*, (Charles H. Ludwig, New York, 1882).

Deane, Frank P., editor, *"My Dear Wife…" The Civil War Letters of David Brett 9th Massachusetts Battery, Union Cannoneer*, (Pioneer Press, Little Rock, 1964).

Dickert, Augustus, *History of Kershaw's Brigade*, (Broadfoot Publishing Co., Wilmington, 1990)

Dunkelman, Mark H. and Michael J. Winey, *The Hardtack Regiment: An Illustrated History of the 154th Regiment, New York State Infantry Volunteers*, (Farleigh Dickinson University Press, Rutherford, 1981).

Elting, John R., *Military Uniforms in America, Long Endure: The Civil War Period, 1852-1867*, (Presidion Press, Novato, 1982)

Fletcher, William A., *Rebel Private Front and Rear*, (Zenger Publishing Co., Inc., Washington D.C., 1985)

Gallagher, Gary W., editor, *The First Day at Gettysburg: Essays on Confederate and Union Leadership*, (Kent State University Press, Kent, 1992)

Gambone, A.M., *The Life of General Samuel K. Zook*, (Butternut and Blue, Gaithersburg, 1996)

Gottfried, Bradley M., *Brigades of Gettysburg, The Union and Confederate Brigades at the Battle of Gettysburg*, (DaCapo Press, Cambridge, 2002)

Hagerty, Edward J., *Collis' Zouaves: The 114th Pennsylvania Volunteers in the Civil War*, (Louisiana State University Press, Baton Rouge, 1997)

Hall, Jeffrey C., *The Stand of the U.S. Army at Gettysburg*, (Indiana University Press, Bloomington, 2003)

The Gettysburg Cyclorama, panel 5

Hard, Abner, *History of the Eighth Cavalry Regiment Illinois Volunteers, During the Great Rebellion*, (Morningside Bookshop, Dayton, 1984)

Hess, Earl J., *Pickett's Charge: The Last Attack at Gettysburg*, (University of North Carolina Press, Chapel Hill, 2001)

Hessler, James A., *Sickles at Gettysburg*, (Savas Beattie, New York, 2009)

Hillyer, George, edited by Gregory Coco, *My Gettysburg Battle Experiences by Captain George Hillyer 9ᵗʰ Georgia Infantry, C.S.A.*, (Thomas Publications, Gettysburg, 2005)

Jones, Terry L., *Cemetery Hill*, (Da Capo Press, Cambridge, 2003)

Jordan, Daniel M., *"Happiness is not My Companion" The Life of General G.K. Warren* (Indiana University Press, Bloomington, 2001)

Jorgensen, Jay, *Gettysburg's Bloody Wheatfield*, (White Mane Books, Shippensburg, 2002)

Kunhardt, Philip B., Jr., *A New Birth of Freedom, Lincoln at Gettysburg*, (Little Brown and Co., Boston, 1983)

Ladd, David L. and Audrey J. Ladd, editors, *The Bachelder Papers*, three volumes, (Morningside Bookshop, Dayton, 1994)

Ladd, David L. and Audrey J. Ladd, editors, *John Bachelder's History of the Battle of Gettysburg*, (Morningside Bookshop, Dayton, 1997)

LaFantasie, Glenn W., *Gettysburg Heroes*, (Indiana University Press, Bloomington, 2008)

LaFantasie, Glenn W., *Twilight at Little Round To*p, (John Wiley & Sons, Hoboken, 2005)

Lamme, Ary J., *America's Historic Landscapes*, (University of Tennessee Press, Knoxville, 1989)

Lasswell, Mary, editor, *Rags and Hope: The Memoirs of Val C. Giles, Four Years with Hood's Brigade, Fourth Texas infantry, 1861-1865*, (Coward-McCann, Inc., New York, 1961)

Leehan, Brian, *Pale Horse at Plum Run: The First Minnesota at Gettysburg*, (Minnesota Historical Society Press, St. Paul, 2002)

Livermore, Thomas L., *Days and Events, 1860-1866*, (Houghton Mifflin Co., Boston, 1920)

The Gettysburg Cyclorama, panel 6

Luvaas, Jay and Harold W. Nelson, editors, *The U.S. Army War College Guide to the Battle of Gettysburg*, (South Mountain Press, Inc., Carlisle, 1986)

Marten, James, *The Children's Civil War*, (University of North Carolina Press, Chapel Hill, 1998)

Matthews, Richard E., *The 149ᵗʰ Pennsylvania Volunteer Infantry Unit in the Civil War*, (McFarland and Co., Jefferson, 1994).

McLean, James L., *Cutler's Brigade at Gettysburg*, (Butternut & Blue, Baltimore, 1994)

McLaughlin, Donald W., *Crossroads of the Conflict: Defining Hours for the Blue and Gray, A Guide to the Monuments of Gettysburg*, (Outskirts Press, Denver, 2008)

Miller, Jerome H., and Delores E. Miller, *Gettysburg for Walkers Only*, (Thomas Publications, Gettysburg, 1991)

Murray, R.L., *"Nothing Could Exceed Their Bravery" New Yorkers in Defense of Little Round Top*, (Benedum Books, Wolcott, 1999)

Murray, R.L., *A Perfect Storm of Lead: George Sears Greene's New York Brigade in Defense of Culp's Hill*, (Benedum Books, Wolcott, 2000)

Murray, R.L., *Letters from Gettysburg: New York Soldiers' Correspondences from the Battlefield*, (Benedum Books, Wolcott, 2005)

Murray, R.L., *Holding the Line: New Yorkers in Defense of Pickett's Charge*, (Benedum Books, Wolcott, 2001)

Murray, R.L., *"Hurrah for the Ould Flag,"* (Benedum Books, New York, 1998)

Murray, R.L., *Letters from Gettysburg: New York Soldiers' Correspendences from the Battlefield*, (Benedum Books, New York, 2005)

Nevins, James H. and William B. Styple, *What Death More Glorious: A Biography of General Strong Vincent*, (Belle Grove Publishing Co., Kearny, 1997)

Newton, Steven H., *McPherson's Ridge: The First Battle for the High Ground, July 1, 1863*, (DaCapo Press, Cambridge, 2002)

Newton, George W., *Silent Sentinels: A Reference Guide to the Artillery at Gettysburg*, (Savas-Beattie, New York, 2005).

Nichols, Edward J., *Toward Gettysburg: A Biography of John F. Reynolds*, (Olde Soldier Books, Gaithersburg, 1987)

The Gettysburg Cyclorama, panel 7

Norton, Oliver W., *The Attack and Defense of Little Round Top*, (Morningside Bookshop, Dayton, 1983)

Penny, Morris M. and J. Gary Laine, *Struggle for the Round Tops*, (Burd Street Press, Shippensburg, 1999)

Persico, Joseph E., *My Enemy My Brother, Men and Days of Gettysburg*, (Collier Books, New York, 1988)

Petruzzi, J. David, *The Complete Gettysburg Guide*, (Savas Beattie LLC, New York, 2009)

Pfanz, Harry W., *Gettysburg—The First Day*, (University of North Carolina Press, Chapel Hill, 2001)

Pfanz, Harry W., *Gettysburg: Culp's Hill & Cemetery Hill*, (University of North Carolina Press, Chapel Hill, 1993)

Report of the New York State Commission, *State of New York Fiftieth Anniversary of the Battle of Gettysburg 1913*, (J.B. Lyon Company, Albany, 1916)

Roach, Harry, *Gettysburg, Hour by Hour*, (Thomas Publications, Gettysburg, 1993)

Sawyer, Franklin, *A Military History of the 8th Ohio Volunteer Infantry*, (reprinted by Blue Acorn Press, Huntington, 1994)

Shue, Richard S., *Morning at Willoughby Run*, (Thomas Publications, Gettysburg, 1998)

Smith, Timothy H., *Farms at Gettysburg, the Fields of Battle*, (Thomas Publications, Gettysburg, 2007)

Styple, William B., editor, *Writing and Fighting the Confederate War, The Letters of Peter Wellington Alexander, Confederate War Correspondent*, (Belle Grove Publishing Co, Kearny, 2002)

Thomas, James E., *The First Day at Gettysburg, A Walking Tour*, (Thomas Publications, Gettysburg, 2005)

Tomasak, Peter, *Avery Harris Civil War Journal*, (Luzerne National Bank, Luzerne, 2000)

Tucker, Phillip T., *Storming Little Round Top*, (Da Capo Press, Cambridge, 2002).

Vanderslice, John M., *Gettysburg Then and Now*, (Morningside Bookshop, Dayton, 1983)

The Gettysburg Cyclorama, panel 8

United States War Department, *The War of the Rebellion: A Compilation of the Official Records of the Union and Confederate Armies*, 70 vols. in 128 parts, (Government Printing Office, Washington D.C., 1880-1901)

Wagner, Richard, *For Honor, Flag and Country: Civil War Major General Samuel W. Crawford, 1827-1892*, (White Mane Books, Shippensburg, 2005)

Ward, Eric, editor, *Army Life in Virginia: The Civil War Letters of George G. Benedict*, (Stackpole Books, Mechanicsburg, 2002)

Wert, Jeffry D., *Gettysburg, Day Three*, (Simon & Schuster, New York, 2001)

Wert, J. Howard, *A Complete Handbook of the Monuments and Indications and Guide to the Positions on the Gettysburg Battlefield*, (R.M. Sturgeon and Co., Harrisburg, 1886)

West, John C., *A Texan in Search of a Fight*, (J.S. Hill and Co., Waco, 1901)

White, Russell C., *The Civil War Diary of Wyman S. White*, (Butternut Blue, Baltimore, 1991)

Winey, Michael J., *Union Army Uniforms at Gettysburg*, (Thomas Publications, Gettysburg, 1998)

Winey, Michael J., *Confederate Army Uniforms at Gettysburg*, (CW Historicals LLC, Collingswood, 2007)

Periodicals
Dunkelman, Mark and Michael J. Winey, "The Hunt for Sergeant Humiston," *Civil War Times Illustrated*, Volume XXI, Number 1, March 1982, p. 28-31.

Dunkelman, Mark H. and Michael J. Winey, "The Hardtack Regiment in the Brickyard Fight," *The Gettysburg Magazine*, Issue Number 8, January 1993, p. 17-30.

Kross, Gary, "Gettysburg Vignettes, Attack from the West," *Blue & Gray Magazine*, Volume XVII, Issue 5, June 2000.

Kross, Gary, "Gettysburg Vignettes, The XI Corps at Gettysburg, July 1, 1863," in *Blue & Gray Magazine*, Volume XIX, Issue 2, December 2001.

Gettysburg Collections
John Bodler Diary

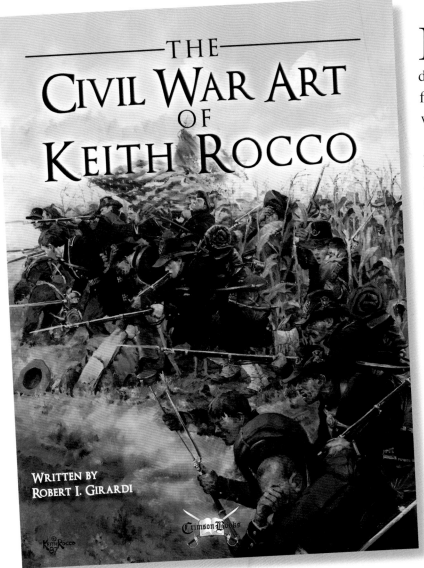